D1723394

Master Your Dopamine:
How to Rewire Your Brain for Focus and Peak Performance

By Nick Trenton
Nicktrenton.com

Table of Contents

CHAPTER 1: WHAT IS DOPAMINE?

The sun is setting over the bustling city, casting a warm orange hue over the skyline. It is a beautiful sight and one that used to bring joy to Jolie every night. But she can't help but feel something else, like there is something missing from her life. Little did she know it is all due to the dysregulation of a little chemical messenger in her brain called dopamine.

Dopamine is a neurotransmitter responsible for regulating emotion and motivation, among other things, such as reward-monitored behavior, working memory, and executive functioning. Having low levels of dopamine can make people feel lethargic and less excited about things, even things that once made them really happy (Dailly, 2004).

Just like Jolie can no longer find joy looking at the sunset even though it used to be one of her favorite things in the world.

But what exactly are neurotransmitters and what do they do? Dopamine is a naturally occurring brain molecule within the body that acts as a neurotransmitter, sending information between neurons (Conrad, 2018). Neurons are nerve cells that make up the nervous system, which consists of the brain and the spinal cord (the central nervous system) as well as nerves that connect to the rest of the body (the peripheral nervous system).

"It's a feel-good molecule," says mental health educator Tanya J. Peterson. It's a part of the reward system, and when the brain creates dopamine in reaction to what people do, they feel good and want to do more of whatever it is that makes them feel as if they are psychologically thriving. This, in turn, leads to increased dopamine production. Thus, dopamine plays an integral role in many of people's most cherished experiences, like the thrill of exciting activities and the joy of connecting with others.

Dopamine is often released when people encounter something pleasurable or rewarding and is a key player in improving their mood and reinforcing behavior patterns. Interestingly, it can even be artificially stimulated by certain drugs that trigger its release. It's no wonder, then, why dopamine has earned its reputation as the *feel good* neurotransmitter; its involvement in amplifying positive moments in people's lives makes them feel great!

When levels of dopamine are low in the brain, people can experience feelings of depression or lethargy, which can lead to an overall lack of motivation or enjoyment in activities (Belujon and Grae, 2017), even ones that once made them happy! Examples of activities that trigger dopamine release include winning a game, learning something new, getting praise from someone important, or enjoying a tasty meal. More recently, research has indicated dopamine may also play a role in addiction and cravings as well as feelings of nostalgia (Oba et al., 2016). In either case, it's clear that dopamine plays an important role in how people experience the world!

The neuroscience of dopamine addiction is fascinating and complex and can be debilitating when individuals become reliant on it. It's like the brain's way of punishing humans for seeking out rewards that aren't necessarily vital for human survival but can often be difficult to "unhook" from—things like drugs, gambling, or compulsive eating. Underneath all these behaviors lie neurochemical reactions that cause some to become addicted by activating pleasure centers and inadvertently reinforcing the behavior of reward-seeking. Understanding the neurochemistry behind this type of addiction can help researchers develop ways to better treat those affected by it.

Current scientific evidence suggests that addiction involves changes to the brain's circuitry on both a psychological and physical level (Kalivas, 2008). These changes mean that the addict is likely to have difficulty with impulse control, emotional regulation, decision-making, and stress management. Furthermore, changes within the reward system are thought to make addictive substances or behaviors more rewarding than other activities, leading to compulsive use despite harmful consequences. Even with advances in this field, understanding addiction neurologically remains difficult, and further research is needed in order to develop effective treatments for those affected by it.

Addiction is increasingly being recognized as a brain illness. Whether it's alcohol, prescription pain pills, cigarettes, gambling, or anything else, resolving an addiction is more complicated than simply stopping or exercising greater control over impulses. Because addiction develops when the pleasure circuits in the brain are overloaded, it can become chronic and even permanent. This is what is meant when individuals read about reward "systems" or "pathways," as well as the significance of dopamine in addiction. But what does it all truly mean?

The reward system, one of the most rudimentary components of the brain, evolved as a means to reinforce survival activities such as feeding or reproducing. When people eat or have sex, the reward pathways release a neurotransmitter called dopamine, which causes a surge of pleasure and satisfaction. This makes them want to do more of those things in the future.

When a person develops an addiction to any substance or behavior, it is because the brain has begun to change. This occurs because addictive substances or behaviors produce an exaggerated response in the brain. They induce dopamine to overwhelm the reward pathways. This surge is vividly remembered by the brain and associated with the addictive substance or behavior, such as drinking or having sex.

However, long-term usage of the chemical causes the brain's circuits to adapt and reduce their sensitivity to dopamine. Achieving that wonderful sensation becomes increasingly vital, but as tolerance builds, people begin to require a greater amount of that substance or activity to achieve the level of high they desire.

Imagine that there is a gatekeeper who controls the release of dopamine. Whenever people experience something rewarding or exciting, the gatekeeper opens the gates and releases that overload of dopamine—just like someone throwing confetti when celebrating a victory! Over time, this continuous release of the feel-good molecule can lead to a sort of "hijacking" of the pleasure centers, whereby even healthy habits no longer provide the same satisfaction that they once did. To break free from addiction long term, it's essential to pay attention to both physiological and psychological elements in order to retrain the brain and create lasting change.

A dopamine detox is a way to help the body rebalance its natural production of dopamine. It usually involves reducing or cutting out processed and sugary foods, as well as making healthy changes to one's lifestyle, such as getting more exercise and engaging in activities like yoga that help reduce stress. Many have found that this kind of detox has greatly improved their mental health and well-being by effectively resetting the brain's chemical messenger system. This can be especially helpful for those with depression, anxiety, or ADHD since balancing dopamine levels is known to improve symptoms in these conditions.

The human brain is a complex network of neurons, and without them, humans wouldn't be the same. Researchers have found dopamine plays an important role in overall cognition by helping people make decisions based on new experiences and triggering feelings of reward when a behavior is successful. In traditional research of rats, a spike of dopamine caused the animal to repeatedly press a lever to obtain a food pellet. This occurs in humans as well—for example, when we choose to consume more tasty food, such as getting another slice of cake. We do this because we end up falling in love with the rewarding feeling the cake initially provided us with, and now we just crave that feeling of reward and satisfaction. Every time we partake in something enjoyable, dopamine is released, lighting up the "satisfaction center" of our brains as it signals a reward is on its way.

This effect helps explain why taking part in seemingly small activities can generate feelings of pleasure and motivation; these events trigger the release of dopamine, thus allowing us to anticipate (and better remember!) rewards. So, while our lives may be too short and days too busy to fully appreciate all the little things, having an understanding of how dopamine operates within this reward prediction framework might be just what we need to make each experience more meaningful!

In a game of chance, researchers looked at the expectation of expecting a payoff. Blood flow in the amygdala and frontal cortex during the anticipation phase (when participants were told they would receive money) indicated activity in the nucleus accumbens and hypothalamus, both of which are abundant in dopamine receptors. The amount of dopamine-driven brain activity was observed to increase as the prospective reward increased (Schultz, 1992).

Furthermore, human bodies are wired to protect us from danger, and the hormone dopamine is an important part of that response. When the brain senses a threat, it instantly floods with dopamine, triggering the fight-or-flight response and allowing people to act quickly in times of danger (Seeman and Seeman, 2014).

This physiological cascade helps us react fast so we can either stand our ground or find the quickest way out! Dopamine acts as an alert signal for our brain to decide whether to prepare for battle or flee from the situation. Once it kicks into gear, it allows us to jump into action and potentially save ourselves; in which case, we should be thankful for the important role of dopamine in the fight-or-flight response! A very helpful little bugger it is!

The Dopamine Loop and Cycle

Talk about the dopamine loop and most minds are likely to wander, imagining excited scientists in a lab somewhere—and science fiction isn't far off with "loops" like this! The reality is that this loop is a key part of the central nervous system. The brain secretes dopamine when it experiences something pleasurable, typically either natural rewards or addictive behaviors. This catches people's attention and motivates them toward repeating them—hence the loop!

A dopamine loop is a behavioral pattern that gives people pleasure through repetition or reward. It's a sequence of events and brain signals stimulated by an external trigger, leading to a pleasurable sensation. A few examples include scrolling through social media, playing video games, or engaging in any type of addictive behavior. Every time people do something that triggers them to get the same reward over and over again, it creates this dopamine loop. These conditions can keep them coming back for more, creating both behavior and thought patterns that are hard to break.

It's an incredibly simple yet powerful concept to explain some of the mechanisms driving people's choices, behaviors, and decisions—from what stimuli entices them the most to how they learn from experiences. Consider going an entire day without using a smartphone or any activity that brings immense joy and constitutes a significant portion of the day. Is it possible to pull off?

Consider Alex and his experience with video games. As an adventurous soul, Alex always looks for new ways to challenge himself and find fulfillment. One day, while wandering around town, he stumbles across an old arcade with classic video games from his childhood lined up in rows. Excited by the idea of playing again, he eagerly drops some coins into one of the machines and begins playing. The thrill of competing against himself brings back memories from long ago; it feels like being a kid again!

As Alex continues to play more games over time, his skill level gradually improves, as well as his confidence in his own abilities. His victories authorize the release of dopamine, which makes him feel even better about winning each game than before. With every success comes greater rewards: higher scores on leaderboards or bragging rights among friends when they play together at home or in online tournaments.

With this newfound sense of accomplishment comes more willingness to take risks and push boundaries; what once seemed impossible now suddenly seems within reach thanks to the dopamine loop's feedback system reinforcing positive behavior through its reward structure. Slowly and gradually, Alex starts to feel down. What once brought him immense joy starts to chip away at him. He is now stuck in a dopamine loop, and it feels like he will never get out of it. Every time he isn't at the arcade, he feels as if he is going insane from pent-up frustration. Every time he isn't at the arcade, *he wants to be*. He craves the thrill, the sense of joy and accomplishment he feels every time he scores high. He craves the sheer nostalgia that playing his childhood favorites brings him.

Unbeknownst to Alex, he has become addicted to the dopamine loop. Some people are masters at moderation. They can devour one square of chocolate or just send one meme to their friends on Instagram before logging out. Those who aren't will have trouble even putting down their phone in the first place.

This is especially true when it comes to controlling social media usage or, in Alex's case, video game activity. Alex's addiction to the dopamine rush manifested as frequent thoughts about going to the arcade, craving the high of achieving something, going to the arcade, check, scroll, read, click, fight, overcome challenges, win a trophy, read, scroll, click, smash, defeat the final boss, win!

It's all too easy to get caught in the loop when there's no moderation. The dopamine loop, it turns out, is the reason for the never-ending rabbit hole Alex and so many people get caught up in. As dopamine is released following pleasure and reward-seeking behaviors, it makes people want them even more. (Have you ever experienced a post-dessert high? Thank dopamine for that.)

The same effect happens when people receive positive social stimulation; that is, when they receive a small reward for browsing through their phone, playing video games, or eating a delicious meal. It creates a loop that makes them want to indulge in the same behavior again and again.

Researcher Kent Berridge postulates that there are two complementary dopamine systems: the "wanting" system and the "liking" system. Dopamine is an essential component of the "wanting" system. It motivates and propels people to take action. The "liking" mechanism helps them feel fulfilled, which causes them to stop looking. However, the dopamine "wanting" system outperforms the "liking" system. People crave more than what they are satisfied with. They can get caught in a dopamine loop. If they don't turn off their "wanting" for a short period of time, they'll find themselves in an infinite loop.

The dopamine "wanting" system is extremely sensitive to "cues" that a reward is on its way. Ivan Pavlov's seminal work on classical conditioning demonstrated the power of anticipation, particularly when it comes to a reward. His experiments showed that dogs can be conditioned to anticipate a reward even in situations lacking an external stimulus. In Pavlov's famous experiment with dogs, the simple act of ringing a bell eventually caused them to become excited and salivate in anticipation of food, even if no food was present.

Similarly, if there is a small, precise hint that something is about to happen, the dopamine system gets activated. If there is a sound or auditory cue (e.g., the sound of an ice cream truck fast approaching) or a visual indication that a notification has arrived (like our phone screen lighting up), the addictive impact is enhanced. The dopamine loop is maintained not by the reward itself, but rather by the anticipation of the reward.

In this hyperconnected world, it's critical to build routines for completely unplugging from social media or moderating a hobby that's bordering on addiction. Overuse of screens has been found in studies to have a bad impact on posture, eyesight, and hearing, and sitting too much can shorten a lifespan by years (Booth et al., 2015). Overuse of smartphones and social networking apps such as Facebook is associated with greater levels of depression and anxiety.

The average smartphone only utilizes about ten applications; any successful app must establish a daily habit in order to entice people into coming back again and again. If people don't keep coming back to an application, it's not really going to be of any benefit to the creators. They need consumers to keep coming and using their apps. Platforms like Snapchat or Instagram have done a good job of keeping people tethered to their bling.

The Hook Model is used by app programmers and user experience designers to accomplish this. It is based on BJ Fogg's study into behavior design at Stanford University and his habit formation model. According to the *Hooked Canvas*, the most successful strategy that social networking apps use to keep people hooked are *variable rewards.* A variable reward is a temporary satisfaction that eventually leaves them wanting more. Autoplay, unlimited scroll, chronological timelines, comments and likes, and automatic push alerts all offer people a steady stream of varied rewards.

These unexpected and often random payoffs are commonly used in the gaming and gambling industries, where unpredictable rewards keep players engaged longer. Contrary to fixed rewards, which remain consistent with each effort, variable rewards offer a more dynamic (and more exciting) experience.

A great example of variable rewards is the slot machine game—people never know how much they will win on each turn. Other examples include fruit machines, scratch cards, or even Instagram—when users scroll through their feed, it's not always clear what types of posts they may find or if an algorithm may boost any particular post to higher visibility. Variable rewards are effective at keeping people's attention because they can't predict the outcome from one interaction to the next, so they keep coming back to try again.

The variable reward of new and fascinating content hooks people in two essential ways for a mega-popular program like Facebook: instant gratification. When people are bored or nervous, Facebook supplies them with a tailored and never-ending stream of new information and entertainment to keep them fully immersed and entertained. The second way is social validation. When they share their own opinions and material with their friends in their social network in the form of status updates and images, they receive social validation in the form of likes, comments, hearts, and shares.

This regular practice of quick fulfillment and social approval generates regular bursts of dopamine. The neural networks in people's brains are rewired to do what makes them feel good and to check their favorite social media apps on a frequent basis as a result of this steady release of dopamine. When they check social media or play a video game, they never know what they're going to get, which is what makes it so addictive and habit building. This is how app builders and game developers keep people firmly planted within the dopamine loop.

Every notification on people's smartphones triggers a dopamine loop that begs to be closed. This is known by psychologists as the Zeigarnik Effect. The psychological temptation to close this loop is frequently too strong to ignore, and before people realize, they've just lost another fifteen minutes of their time because of a single notification. This dopamine loop is challenging to break because of the combination of dopamine release in the brain and a conditioned reaction with motor movement (the swipe with a finger or thumb, or the pressing of the buttons on a joystick).

When it comes to motivation that drives behavior, dopamine often plays a major role (Freed, 2022). As it turns out, dopamine is much more heavily released by anticipation of the reward than reward itself (Pearce, 2019). To put this in perspective, a lot of people may be more likely to stay up late preparing for an upcoming party than they are to actually enjoy the event itself!

Another example would be if someone was on their way to do something they'd been waiting and wanting to do for quite some time; the bodily sensation of excitement and anticipation is often accompanied by the release of dopamine. That's why people often get more joy from planning for activities rather than actually doing them! The "wanting" part is often stronger than the "liking" part.

This phenomenon can be seen in other areas of life as well, such as when people are awaiting a birthday or Christmas gift. All the build up to that day creates a feeling of excitement and joy that usually surpasses the moment the gifts are unwrapped. The same can also be found in winning a competition or game; the long wait to hear who won, especially if there are several contestants, is nerve-wracking but always worth it in the end. It's true that anticipation can sometimes supersede the pleasure of finally receiving what was wanted. It doesn't feel as thrilling anymore. It is the feeling of "wanting" and anticipation that sustains the dopamine loop.

This is why people obsessively monitor their social media feeds for fear of missing out on something intriguing, and why they constantly shape their social media identities by uploading fresh content in order to gain additional social approval in the form of comments and likes. As a result of all of this, they invest their time and energy in creating these social identities on their platforms, allowing social media behemoths to better understand their preferences and passions. These platforms in turn create an algorithm that shows them enticing offers and ads that make them come back again and again in hopes of finding something new.

Dopamine and Addiction

The cold sweat on her forehead and the pounding of her heart are unmistakable signs that Emily is addicted. She had been drawn in by the tantalizing promise of reward, an escape from her mundane life into a world where anything seems possible. But little does she know, as she partakes in activities to feed this addiction, that dopamine and its associated reward centers are actually playing a huge role in driving it forward.

It started with innocent online gaming, something to pass the time when boredom set in. But soon enough, Emily finds herself needing ever more intense thrills to satisfy her cravings for stimulation and pleasure— no longer content with simply beating levels or completing tasks within games. Instead, she begins taking risks—betting heavily on virtual gambling sites or investing enormous amounts of money into stocks, hoping for large returns overnight—all fueled by the brain's desire for rewards based on the dopamine release from engaging in activities like these.

Before long, though, Emily finds herself facing dire financial troubles as a result of these reckless pursuits and has begun losing control over them completely. She can't bring herself to stop even if she wants to because she is stuck in what psychologists call "a dopamine trap."

It is truly incredible how the human brain works. Recent advances in neuroscience have enabled us to understand the scientific implications behind what was once just speculation. Through extensive research, psychologists now refer to addiction as "a dopamine trap"—essentially, the mind is trained to actively seek out and reward itself with dopamine through substance use or behaviors like gambling.

Engaging in pleasurable activities can produce a powerful chemical reaction within the brain that triggers feelings of euphoria and contentment, sometimes even referred to as "chasing a high." People can become addicted to the wonderful feelings they experience when they engage in rewarding activities.

Yet, recovering from addiction is anything but easy; people's minds can be incredibly powerful motivators when it comes to trying to obtain rewards like those generated by addicting activities. The dopamine released during these moments creates a tempting positive reinforcement loop—a beautiful illusion of reward often leading them down darker paths. When experts refer to addiction as being "a dopamine trap," they are speaking in earnest.

People's brains adjust when they are regularly exposed to the stimuli that make them happy, and eventually they require more and more of those stimuli just to feel "normal" or pain-free. The loop that brings them there is known as a "dopamine deficit state," and it can actually cause melancholy, anxiety, irritability, and insomnia. The brain's circuits change over time and gradually become less sensitive to dopamine. Gaining access to that enjoyable feeling becomes more and more crucial, but at the same time, the brain's tolerance grows and requires progressively more of that substance or activity to achieve the desired high.

It's crucial to engage in dopamine-releasing activities on a regular basis for the sake of feeling good, but it's critical to avoid becoming dependent on the release. It's possible to have too much of a good thing, as the adage goes, and this is true for dopamine as well. Dopamine may cause problems for people who have trouble with moderation. Let's examine what dependence on a dopamine high can entail and explore some examples of risky dopamine-releasing activities.

Sex makes people feel good and releases dopamine. This can result in an inability to exert control over sexual thoughts, cravings, and impulses, which is referred to as sex addiction. Although sexual urges are natural, sex addiction only refers to actions that are excessive and have a substantial detrimental impact on one's life.

Someone suffering from sex addiction may find themselves thinking about sex all the time. They're stuck in dopamine's "wanting" system and constantly crave and anticipate the pleasure that comes with sexual arousal and engaging in sexual activities. These recurring sexual ideas or fantasies might become compulsive or interfere with other tasks. The dopamine "high" becomes so sought after that a person might even put themselves in danger just to get their fix.

Since sex is so pleasurable, a person may be inclined to indulge in it again and again, thus maintaining their dopamine loop. According to research, it is not uncommon for those who are sexually compulsive to simultaneously exhibit symptoms of melancholy, anxiety, and social anxiety (Weiss, 2010).

Food addiction is characterized by binge eating, cravings, and a lack of control over food. Food is tasty, and that means consuming it results in a dopamine rush that fills people up with immense pleasure and satisfaction. Indeed, research indicates that the impact of food addiction on the brain's reward and control pathways are similar to those of addictive substances (Adams et al., 2019). Cravings occur frequently, and gratifying or ignoring them becomes difficult. These cravings are caused by the brain's desire for something that releases dopamine. If people notice that their cravings are consuming them, they seem to be always preoccupied with satisfying them even when they're not even hungry in the first place. It's likely that they might have developed a food addiction.

Additionally, dopamine plays a major role in alcohol and substance use disorders. The brain releases dopamine during activities it perceives as positive or rewarding, and those with a substance use disorder experience an exaggerated release of dopamine when engaging in the behaviors associated with their substance of choice. For example, cocaine, opioids, and alcohol all produce a dramatic pleasurable surge of dopamine. This reaction encourages these individuals to repeat the behavior despite negative consequences, making it difficult to break free from dependence on alcohol or substances.

A telltale sign of a substance addiction is when people continue to take prescription drugs after they are no longer essential to treat a health concern. For example, after undergoing major surgery and being prescribed opioids to manage pain, they continue to take them even after the prescription period ends.

Chapter Takeaways:

- Dopamine is a naturally occurring brain chemical that functions as a neurotransmitter, transmitting information between neurons. It's part of the reward system, and when the brain produces dopamine in response to something, people feel good.
- People feeling good in response to something results in enhanced dopamine production. As a result, dopamine plays an important role in many of people's most treasured experiences. Examples of activities that trigger dopamine release include

winning a game, learning something new, getting praise from someone important, or enjoying a tasty meal.

- A dopamine loop is just a way to describe how our brains react to rewards. Whenever we do something that gives us pleasure, like eating our favorite type of food or playing a game, the reward system in our brain kicks in and releases a chemical called dopamine. This process creates an intense feeling of pleasure, but it also serves as motivation for us to keep doing that same activity over and over again, hence the "loop" part of the term. Some classic examples of dopamine loops would be gambling, shopping, and playing video games, all activities where people often find themselves unable to stop consistently engaging even when they don't really want to participate anymore!

- A dopamine addiction is an unhealthy dependence on certain behaviors that are associated with the release of dopamine in the brain. It can manifest itself as seeking frequent thrills like gambling, having sex, or taking drugs, or repeatedly doing something for pleasure without thinking about the repercussions of the actions.

- A dopamine detox is a method of rebalancing the body's natural production of the feel-good neurotransmitter. It usually entails decreasing or eliminating processed and sugary meals, as well as making healthy lifestyle adjustments such as getting more exercise and participating in stress-relieving activities such as yoga.

CHAPTER 2: HOW TO DEAL WITH A DOPAMINE ADDICTION—THE DOPAMINE DETOX

The dopamine detox, or dopamine fasting, is a concept coined in 2019 by California-based psychiatrist Dr. Cameron Sepah (Gepp, 2021). A dopamine fast tries to "reset your dopamine levels" by urging individuals to refrain from anything that gives them pleasure—for starters, smartphones, social media, Netflix, cheat meal food, and even sex.

Such an approach could potentially help reduce dopamine state cravings and help cut down on excessive internet usage, as well as restore balance in areas such as work productivity and social relationships overall. He postulates that, "Dopamine fasting is a technique to manage addictive behaviors, by restricting them to specific periods and practicing fasting from impulsively engaging in them, in order to regain behavioral flexibility."

Sepah's unique approach to dopamine detoxing focuses on individualized behavior modification versus traditional prohibition of all technology. This is beneficial in that it allows the participant to decide which behaviors are unhealthy and ought to be restricted, and which may be manageable. Striving to gain control of seemingly unstoppable unhealthy stimuli like social media, online sales ads, pornography, and gambling promotions is no easy feat. By helping individuals identify when their mind and body is heading down a negative path, Sepah's method provides tools that allow people to make a conscious effort to take back control from these triggers.

Sepah only promotes restriction if it has been properly shown to cause distress and to negatively impact other areas of life such as career or relationships, and when individual attempts at cutting out the behavior have failed. This form of dopamine fasting emphasizes the importance of accepting challenging emotions like boredom or loneliness, rather than turning to quick solutions or activities that could become addictive in nature.

He hopes that his strategy will help people combat obsessive behaviors and acquire control over the continual barrage of toxic impulses in their lives. But it can certainly be very hard for individuals to battle addictions.

Since a dopamine detox involves removing oneself from common stimulants like social media, candy, and shopping and abandoning them in favor of behaviors and lifestyle decisions that are less impulsive, it can be really hard for people to stop themselves from wanting and then indulging. **To make dealing with these "wanting" urges and impulses easier, Sepah relies on cognitive behavioral therapy (CBT) as a foundation for his practice.** CBT is an evidence-based technique that focuses on identifying and changing negative thoughts and behaviors in order to promote more positive coping strategies.

He incorporates mindfulness practices to assist people in breaking bad behaviors, such as advising them to sit with their impulses rather than acting on them right away. This behavior is widely **used in CBT and is referred to as "urge surfing,"** attributed to psychologist Dr. Alan Marlatt. For instance, it can be highly effective in helping people accept and cope with feelings of boredom and loneliness that often result when individuals refrain from impulsively indulging. The premise here is that if people learn how to just be themselves without having to act upon every urge, they'll be able to successfully regulate their dopamine levels.

During the practice of **urge surfing**, individuals learn to ride out psychological cravings, much like a surfer rides out a wave. First, they acknowledge the craving (I am having the thought that I want cigarettes), remembering that it will eventually subside. Then they label their emotions (frustration, anxiety upon not having it), noting any physical sensations in their body that accompany the emotions (sweating, rapid heartbeat, elevated temperature) while using other mindfulness practices such as deep breathing. By immersing themselves in the present moment, they are able to gain new perspectives on their mental states and make more informed decisions about how to respond to difficult thoughts and feelings. With regular practice, this technique can be a powerful tool for managing unwanted or unhealthy urges in daily life and ultimately help in naturally increasing sensitivity to dopamine.

CBT involves understanding the relationship between our thoughts, feelings, and behaviors while also engaging in activities that help reframe our thinking from negative to more positive or neutral perspectives. For example, individuals might challenge themselves to identify the potential benefits of boredom, such as increased creativity or focus for an upcoming task. Loneliness, on the other hand, might be addressed by instilling a sense of connectedness via meaningful self-care practices such as journaling or expressing gratitude for simple pleasures that don't require physical interaction with others.

Individuals who are adept at distracting their thoughts or performing an unrelated action when an urge arises (Azrin and Nunn, 1977) may successfully suppress the urge without completely feeling its intensity. This will prevent them from truly experiencing its severity. Urge surfing does not mean that individuals have to fight the urge and make it go away. Instead, they learn how to completely experience the urge in a different way, which is to experience the urge for what it is: brief, nonlethal, with a generally predictable path, and most importantly, defeatable.

Sepah identifies six compulsive behaviors that might be restricted during a dopamine detox, including comfort eating, excessive online activity, gambling, shopping, porn, and recreational drugs. Despite the deceptive name, the dopamine fasting plan focuses on confronting undesirable behaviors rewarded by dopamine rather than lowering dopamine itself. He believes that by avoiding the instant gratification that these items provide, people can attain more rewarding long-term goals/gratification and liberate themselves from painful or time-consuming compulsions that provide only instant dopamine hits.

Stimulus Control

Taking control of repetitive, habitual behaviors during a dopamine fast can be a challenging prospect. In order to achieve this, another CBT technique known as "stimulus control" can prove to be an immensely valuable strategy. Stimulus control refers to instances in which a behavior is elicited by the presence or absence of a stimulus. If a person always eats while watching TV, eating behavior is influenced by the stimulus of watching TV. A student may be talkative with friends yet quiet in class because the social environment is exerting stimulus control over talking. Stimulus control has the ability to either encourage or inhibit behavior.

In studies, it has been observed that when reinforcement or reward—such as food or money—is given out at random intervals to a subject, it increases their dopamine levels more than reward doled out on a predictable schedule (Schultz, 1993). Thus, by controlling the stimuli of food or money, individuals can successfully regulate their dopamine levels. This is because the brain craves surprise and stimulation, encouraging people to search for something new. If a person watches TV while having dinner every night, this routine is gradually going to decrease their sensitivity to dopamine (as there is no modification in the stimuli, and dopamine craves novelty), and they'll require more of the same behavior (more TV hours and more food) to achieve the same high.

Over time, the brain is designed to identify and modify the factors that cause and reinforce such behavior in order to direct circumstances toward a new, healthier behavior pattern. Stimulus control involves ordering one's environment in a way that eliminates opportunities for negative behaviors by removing harmful stimuli (removing the TV) from the surrounding environment and instead encourages desirable outcomes to occur naturally. *Thus, encouraging the regulation of dopamine naturally by discouraging immediate gratification.*

Everyone loves the feeling of immediate gratification—that sense of accomplishment upon reaching a goal or completing a task at hand. The problem with short-term gratification is that it can often come with short-term consequences, too, making people more likely to fall into bad habits. Long-term gratification, on the other hand, takes a little more commitment and effort but has lasting rewards. Taking the time to invest in the future, for example, whether through studying for exams or working hard for a goal body, can provide individuals with immense satisfaction. The joy and happiness are also more long lasting, hence more dopamine.

For example, removing the TV from a place where an individual normally dines can help keep their overeating habits in check. This makes it an effective tool for creating lasting and significant progress in overturning old tendencies and helping people avoid indulging in harmful behaviors during a dopamine fast. Here's how stimulus control works:

If someone always drinks while playing video games, the stimulus of video games is what regulates their drinking behavior. (This may be a crucial realization for certain people, as people don't often realize how their unhealthy habits are being encouraged by things they consider normal). *If the main goal of their dopamine fast is to refrain from drinking, they'd have to get rid of the video games and the TV (harmful stimuli) in order to successfully complete their fast and make it a little easier on their willpower.* If there's chocolate at home, nobody is going to eat any right? (At least not easily).

This control of harmful stimuli is also going to cause their dopamine levels to increase naturally, as the brain craves change. And it shifts from immediate gratification to long term, the brain's reward centers will be constantly engaged, contributing to better satisfaction and resourcefulness long term.

If a person finds themselves frequently distracted by their cell phone, they may choose to put it away or make it harder to access. This will reduce their temptation and help them stay focused on tasks that require their full attention. It can take a little bit of extra effort at first, but eventually people who practice stimulus control will find that it becomes much easier and more beneficial over time. This will make their dopamine fast goals easier to accomplish.

People can also set up their phone's own built-in timer to pull them out of the never-ending loop of scrolling through social media apps. Some apps like Instagram even came up with a feature that lets them track their activity and set up a timer that goes off when they cross the limit they have set for themselves. They can also block and restrict which notification they want to receive.

According to Carol Vidal, an assistant professor of psychiatry and behavioral sciences at Johns Hopkins University, "Excessive technology use can take time away from things such as sleep, exercise, and socializing, which are all crucial for well-being."

Given the burgeoning ubiquity of technology in day-to-day life, for most people, ditching it altogether isn't going to happen. As such,

Miguel Vidal suggests *cutting down as a more realistic approach*. To do this, it is imperative to formulate an action plan. Identify unhealthy habits and then decide which elements to focus on; a great starting point would be assessing one's usage pattern and where time is allocated amongst different applications.

For example, an unhealthy habit could be excessive drinking. An important element could be that the person drinks excessively only when gaming. This will help in connecting the dots and eliminating stimuli that are encouraging that behavior. Conclusively, this will make the dopamine fast way easier than it would have been had the gaming console constantly beckoned one with its shiny glory.

Furthermore, Dr. George advises setting limits and deleting anything that makes one feel worse or stressed out, but of course, what constitutes healthy utilization is subjective and highly dependent on individual needs. Taking regular breaks from screens throughout the day can help people manage stress and remain productive.

Scheduling specific times for these breaks on their calendars can be a great way of ensuring they don't get lost in the digital world and neglect themselves. Setting an alarm on their phone is also another reliable way to be prompted when it's time to step away, no matter where they are or what they're doing. Once their break starts, they need to make sure to put away any devices and fully disengage so that they can truly relax and reset their mind.

People need to start by determining their dopamine diet and how much time they want to devote to the information source (persona "information diet") in a particular day or week. Are they okay with an hour, a day, or only fifteen minutes? Then, determine which outlets to prioritize. There is no right or wrong; what counts is that their behavior corresponds to their objective. For example, people could set aside thirty minutes each day for watching the news or reading a newspaper. Put a timer on their phone for the set amount of time. As soon as it goes off, immediately stop.

Next, choose a time and location where they prefer to read the news. Fortunately, many people now are working from home, making habits easy to establish. Take advantage of it! Choosing a consistent time and location will help their brand-new habit persist. For instance, a person can choose to read the news or a magazine on your couch for thirty minutes after lunch.

If there's one thing people have learned over the past year, it's that social media can be draining, and people often find themselves comparing their lives to others, a habit that takes away from their own energy. That's why it might be worthwhile to take a step back and unfollow some accounts that are doing more harm than good. Lastly, do not forget to set a timer. This might feel like a little too much, but it will help in honoring that time limit.

"Social media use can exacerbate mental health problems," says Heidi Faust, LCSW, a licensed therapist at Thriveworks. If people find themselves having negative emotions or compulsions to obsessively check your social media accounts, regardless of the terrible emotions it causes, it may be time to shake things up."

Multi-tasking and trying to do too many things all at once can be highly stressful. For those feeling stressed, it might be valuable to engage in an alternative activity that is incompatible with whatever is causing the stress (the stimulus); this could mean doing something physical instead of sitting in front of a screen all day, or going outdoors for some fresh air and sunshine instead of worrying about satisfying that "urge to indulge."

There are some itches that shouldn't be scratched. Think of the urge as an "itch." If it is constantly scratched, it might get infected. *The dopamine system works in a similar fashion. Continuously satisfying an urge is going to make it come back stronger than ever, and it's going to require an individual to scratch a lot harder.* If someone is addicted to the dopamine high that accompanies a good meal and is always ready to indulge in a little emotional eating, it would be beneficial to go and play badminton instead as soon as the urge surfaces. This is the backbone of a dopamine fast—replace all harmful behaviors with healthy ones and *do not give in to the urge.*

Similarly, if someone is craving their next drug fix, it would be pertinent that they go swimming or biking instead. Physical activity also authorizes the release of dopamine and helps revamp and remodel the reward system over time, resulting in increased circulating amounts of dopamine and more accessible dopamine receptors. Exercise can do both—alleviate depression and increase your capacity for joy. These adjustments can also help to repair the brain damage caused by substance abuse. Substance addiction affects dopamine levels in the brain and the availability of dopamine receptors in the reward system. As a result, addicts may feel unmotivated, sad, antisocial, and unable to appreciate regular joys. Exercise can help to reverse this.

In addition to that, consider limiting sources of consumption and information. Most people, when prompted, can't remember ever feeling so compelled to continually check the news as they have in the last two years, or endlessly scroll on social media. This disastrous mix of risk and economical uncertainty, and the rapid development of the COVID-19 pandemic, created a unique desire in everyone to stay up to date nearly to the minute.

This underlines the obvious fact that news is both informative and entertaining. One major reason people become addicted to the news is that news websites and apps function similarly to slot machines, providing them with a new burst of dopamine each time they "pull to refresh." In case people decide to limit the amount of needless information they consume, here are a few basic steps to take:

By setting up a firewall, either on one's computer or other device such as a tablet, a person can block themselves from accessing certain websites that may provide bad temptations—e.g., a person is working and all these porn ads keep popping up (harmful stimuli), and it'll be hard to resist the urge of just abandoning their dopamine fast and giving in to the dopamine high. Not only will this limit the ability to search for potentially prohibited material but it will also help keep distractions away. With social accountability, people can have friends or family members hold them accountable by monitoring their progress and being there for support; this can help reduce anxiety and stress associated with compulsions.

Lastly, counseling should be sought if available; professional counselors can provide motivation and insight while offering structure and guidance throughout the recovery process. Seeking support from family, friends, or support groups can further buoy motivation and resolve when feeling overwhelmed by the challenge at hand. Both patience and determination are essential for long-term success, as dopamine addiction takes time to wean off from.

The Fasting Schedule

As already established, every time someone goes through Instagram, watches something on YouTube or Netflix, gets likes on a Facebook post, plays *The Last of Us*, or takes a bite of a juicy hamburger, their brain releases a large amount of the neurochemical dopamine. With time, their sensitivity to dopamine decreases and they require more of the chemical to achieve the same high. They'll eat more fast food, play more video games, or spend copious amounts of time on social media.

This is where Sepah's dopamine fast comes into play. A little recap: dopamine fasting is the practice of avoiding things that are gratifying and joyful in an addictive sense in order to break addictive behavior and reset the neurochemical dopamine—think compulsively checking phones or aimlessly scrolling while at dinner with friends.

So, how does dopamine fasting work?

Taking the time to engage in self-care can be immensely rewarding and beneficial to well-being, but it's important to find what works best for individual needs. Utilizing a technical approach and setting aside one to four hours at the end of the day (depending on personal and professional demands) to completely abstain from all addictive behaviors. No electronics (phone, Netflix, laptop, video games, etc.), no reading books or magazines, no sex or masturbation, no food, no talking, no music or podcasts, no coffee or other stimulants.

Writers often travel to secluded places and with limited access to the modern's world's amenities. This helps them energize and recharge and get their thoughts and ideas organized without any interruption from the *ding-ding-ding* of everyday life. This is akin to a dopamine fast.

Activities that individuals can allow themselves to partake in could include: writing (with pen and paper), meditating, going for walks, doing some deep thinking, inner child-work, visualizing, and replenishing with water. Individuals can devote one weekend day (spent outdoors on a Saturday or Sunday), one weekend per quarter (go on a trip), or one week per year (go on vacation!).

These are suggested guidelines that help structure healthy and enriching activities. However, if committing so much time is difficult to manage, then start with dopamine fasting for one hour per day or whatever might be easier and more sustainable long term. Ultimately, don't overthink it; take small achievable steps and simply focus on doing something that energizes the mind, body, and soul. The key here is to take a set amount of time and abstain from all activities that are joyful in an addictive sense.

Develop a fasting schedule, as it can be an effective way to regain control over problematic behavior while still engaging in it periodically. By designating certain days and times when the behavior is allowed, individuals can create structure and boundaries that will allow them to ultimately become more flexible with their choices. This strategy is especially relevant when considering associated behaviors, such as late nights, weekends, and vacations, as the fasting schedule limits their engagement to a level that helps sustain balance. It is important to note that a fasting schedule requires conscious effort; strong implementation is essential for success.

Here's a straightforward three-step process.

Identify your biggest distractions. Once you have identified the activities that are your biggest distractions and temptations by practicing an exposure exercise (detailed in the previous section), it is time to create an action plan to help manage them. This can be done on paper or in a document dedicated for this purpose. Divide the document into two sections, Can and Cannots. Under each section, list the activities you can still engage in, such as exercising, reading books, taking a walk, or painting, and list the activities you should avoid while undergoing detoxification, such as checking emails, using your computer, or using social media. Knowing what you should and shouldn't do will make it easier to stay focused during the detox period.

In assistance, consider asking the following questions: "Which one of the following would significantly increase my attention and productivity if I stopped doing only one thing?" "What other activities should I avoid in order to dramatically improve my focus?" Continue to pose these questions until fully satisfied with the responses. Put the completed list on the desk or wherever else it will be noticed. It will serve as a useful reminder of the activities that should be avoided. Furthermore, an individual can also make use of colorful sticky notes and jot down these lists onto them. Paste them around the room or stick them onto their bathroom mirror. It'll surely not be missed there.

Adding friction to the environment can help people achieve their goals and battle undesirable behaviors. Friction is simply making something less accessible and easier to avoid, while also making more desirable behaviors easier to pursue. For instance, if an individual struggles with eating junk food, it makes sense to move any snacks away from the living room—make them difficult to access—while keeping healthy options right in front of them at all times. It's a simple way to outmaneuver the ingrained habits by disrupting the process just enough so that it takes more effort to repeat it. In this case, an individual is breaking the cycle of bad snacking by adding an extra step! This is what controlling harmful stimuli (stimulus control) is about.

Distractions can be a major challenge when it comes to staying focused with one's goals.

In order to increase the likelihood of success, individuals need to introduce some practical friction into the equation. For instance, if your phone is typically a big source of distraction, turn off notifications or even put it on airplane mode. If you're constantly drawn to Facebook, try removing as many notifications as possible and investing in applications like News Feed Eradicator that help keep you on track. Lastly, if YouTube keeps getting the best of you, install an app that can reduce distractions by eliminating all the extraneous content (like suggestions and recommendations). Ultimately, it's about turning off automatic options and having a concrete purpose for consuming entertainment; only watch videos when they serve a purposeful role.

Adding friction to a task can be an incredibly successful way of changing our behavior. Humans tend to come up with the path of least resistance, and if you give us more work or make it difficult, we won't often go the extra mile. Take Jace's internet modem situation: instead of having it easily visible in plain sight and just turning it on, he put it in his storage room instead. He thinks this will help him stay away from playing around online during the day; he doesn't just have to turn it on, but in order to get to it, he also has to trek out there and turn it on, adding two layers of intentional difficulty to using the internet! In the end, all these added frictions definitely change his behavior, which is exactly what he wants at the end of the day.

If someone is dealing with a food addiction, they can start by removing junk and snacks from plain sight (friction 1). They can further hide that junk up on the highest shelf of their pantry (Friction 2) so that there is one more hurdle between them and the junk. This will demotivate them, and they are less likely to indulge and maintain their dopamine fast.

Everyone knows it can be hard to focus on their goals and stay away from undesired behaviors. But it's really just about finding the best way to set up conditions that make it easier for people to stick with their plan. For example, some people like to start their mornings off with a writing session. To make sure they don't procrastinate, they open their word processor before checking emails or scrolling through their phone. Plus, some listen to calming music while they work in forty-five-minute bursts with a timer running; this means they won't get sidetracked midsession and feel disappointed if they have to stop what they're doing. This way, by avoiding any extra "friction," their mind is much more inclined to follow along and keep working toward their goals!

So, how can one create friction to eliminate unwanted behaviors? Take a look at the Cannots list. Make a list of specific things that can be done to cause friction next to each of them. After that, review the list of Cans and make a list of things one could do to reduce friction. Remember that the mind is lazy. It's best if that fact is used to one's benefit.

Begin first thing in the morning. Starting the day with a great foundation is one of the surest ways to achieve success. Simply beginning the day off right can help set the tone for how we'll tackle the day ahead. The third and final step to starting is just, well, starting! Meurisse suggests tackling an important task first thing in the morning without checking our phones or distracting ourselves with social media. Creating a morning routine that includes rituals such as breakfast, exercise, journaling, or meditation will also provide us with focus and greater clarity when it comes time to take action. In the long term, this simple commitment can have vast impacts on one's life both personally and professionally.

Waking up in the morning can sometimes be tricky, but setting a routine can help make it easier. The key is to establish something that boosts our focus and concentration instead of overstimulating us. Writing down two or three simple things we can do each morning can lay the foundation for our day and help focus our mind and body with activities like meditating, stretching, or listening to some relaxation music. Even just writing down three things we're grateful for or repeating positive mantras before launching into the day can give us a sense of balance and positivity. It's important to identify what will work best for you so that the routine becomes part of an enriching experience that nurtures our mental and physical health.

Now that we have identified the biggest temptations and/or distractions, written them down on a piece of paper, made sure that the paper is somewhere it can always be seen, added friction to the Cannots by making unwanted behaviors harder to engage in, and implemented a daily routine to calm the mind and start with low-level stimulation, we can choose whether we want to detox for forty-eight hours, twenty-four hours, or for part of the time.

Next, we need to decide which primary stimulation sources we'll cut out as we go through our detox. Consider eliminating most, if not all, sources of stimulation throughout the forty-eight- and twenty-four-hour detoxes. Avoid using the internet. Halt the gambling. Don't watch TV. Put an end to the incessant gaming. Eat small unprocessed and sugar-free meals. Turn off the phone. Try to get rid of all primary source(s) of distraction during the dopamine detox.

The Feasting Schedule

Now that the fast is over, it's time for some feasting! People find themselves routinely doing something they'd like to minimize.

Maybe they're checking their phone more often than they'd like, or engaging in a habit that's not helpful to them health-wise. To help reduce the amount of time spent on this behavior, utilizing a feasting schedule could be a great idea. Allowing ourselves to engage in the behavior for short windows throughout the day—such as checking our phone five to thirty minutes after each mealtime—can aid in controlling how much we're doing it and when.

This method can provide structure while allowing occasional indulgence. We can ask ourselves what behaviors we are looking to spend less time on. A bit of time restriction could be just the thing we need to help set boundaries and have lasting results.

Allowing the activity to take place a few times per day, with time limits lasting between five to thirty minutes, is a great way to incorporate the desirable activity in conscious moderation. For example, playing video games for an hour per day after work. Or indulging your palette with fast food only once a week or every other week. It's fine to eat nutritious foods during a dopamine fast—just avoid extremely rewarding/addictive items like refined carbs, salty chips, and sugary treats.

When it comes to internet use and video games, avoid anything designed by a company (movies/television) or requiring frequent input (scrolling/clicking), because such goods prioritize user engagement over user well-being. While the internet can be a terrific tool for learning, the frequent attentional switching (and hence dopaminergic firing) from social media, publications, forums, games, and so on is what is problematic. If something generates an emotion that is both high in energy/arousal and very positive in quality/valence (such as euphoria or anxiety), consider regulating internet use even during the feasting period.

Implementing this technique with your phone use habits can be done by allowing yourself to check for notifications and communications only after mealtimes for a brief moment before concluding and moving on. This new habit allows the user to control their consumption or usage of their device without feeling overly restricted from engaging with it.

Chapter Takeaways:

- Sepah's dopamine detox promotes a more mindful approach to technology consumption that includes staying away from screens and leisure activities, such as shopping, music streaming, and gaming, for short periods of time whilst also refraining from doing things impulsively in order to reclaim behavioral flexibility.
- Stimulus control is a behavior therapy strategy that helps recognize and manage external stimuli, such as environmental cues, that may influence people's thoughts and behaviors. It entails becoming aware of specific variables that may trigger habits or negative feelings, then altering those conditions wherever possible to allow people to respond to desired behavior more effectively.
- The brain adjusts when people are regularly exposed to the stimuli that makes them happy—with the brain circuits gradually becoming less

sensitive to dopamine. Eventually, people require more and more of those stimuli just to feel normal. For example, sex makes people feel good and releases dopamine. This can result in an inability to exert control over sexual thoughts, cravings, and impulses, which is referred to as sex addiction.

- To practice dopamine fasting, utilize a technical approach and set aside one to four hours at the end of the day to completely abstain from all addictive behaviors. No electronics (phone, Netflix, laptop, or video games), no reading books or magazines, no sex or masturbation, no food, no talking, no music or podcasts, no coffee or other stimulants.

- To help reduce the amount of time spent on an addictive behavior, utilizing a feasting schedule could be a great idea. Allowing people to engage in the behavior for short windows throughout the day—such as checking their phone five to thirty minutes after each mealtime—can aid in controlling how much they're doing it and when.

CHAPTER 3: THE ROLE OF DOPAMINE IN INTERNAL DRIVE AND MOTIVATION

DOPAMINE AND DECISION-MAKING

Dopamine is also directly linked to people's sense of motivation. It can help them focus more deeply and decrease their threshold for taking action toward specific goals. To put it simply, when the dopamine levels are high, people prefer to focus their attention on exterior goals, the things they want, and feel driven to seek them. "Dopamine is about wanting, not having," states Dr. Anna Lembke, a professor of psychiatry and behavioral sciences at Stanford University. When dopamine levels are low, people become unmotivated, experience less pleasure from activities, and become physically weary (Huberman, 2022).

One of the most significant questions in neuroscience surrounds how decisions are made and behavior is controlled. Dopamine is essential in all of this. Researchers from the Technical University of Munich (TUM) and the Max Planck Institute of Neurobiology investigated the role that dopamine plays in decision-making and motor control.

Certain scents and flavors are innately appealing to animals. Alluring aromas are associated with things like delicious food. Less appealing scents, such as rotten food, immediately send the animal a signal that indicates "There could be trouble here!" All animals have similar taste preferences when it comes to food: Sugars and fats are pleasantly viewed, but bitter tastes are negatively regarded.

In order to be able to make such judgments, humans require signals from the brain that tell us "This is good" or "This is terrible." The dopaminergic system in the brain, often known as the reward system, is involved in these assessments. The dopaminergic system is a complex network involving various regions of the brain. It primarily functions to regulate motivation, movement, and reward-related behavior. It receives dopaminergic signals from neurons in the ventral tegmental area (VTA) and projects them to various pathways in the brainstem and forebrain that influence a range of cognitive processes; it is also known to have direct impacts on areas such as memory, decision-making, and attention.

Dopaminergic neurons use varied activity patterns to deliver a signal to the brain about what the body requires and senses. Researchers were able to demonstrate that the functioning of a network of dopaminergic neurons mirrors both the organism's natural preferences for taste and smell as well as its physiological status (Acharya and Shukla, 2012). Dopaminergic neurons store information about whether or not an organism is moving in addition to sensory cues like smell or taste. Neurons can react to both internal behavioral states and external impulses, combining them to enable cognitive and motor functions.

"By doing that, the neurons can react flexibly and individually to the most important information, such as smell, taste, but also hunger or one's own movement. This is important to reach a balanced decision, because an external sensory signal can sometimes mean something good or bad, depending on an organism's condition," explains Prof. Grunwald Kadow.

So, what does this mean for decision-making? According to research, dopamine influences how people choose between immediate rewards versus things that might occur in the future (Schultz, 2004). In other words, it forces individuals to focus on the here and now rather than how their spur-of-the-moment decisions may influence them in the future. This can lead them toward making unhealthy choices.

Consider this: This dopaminergic system releases dopamine into the brain when people experience something pleasurable. When individuals are presented with choices, that pleasure or reward can be used to determine which choice will be made. The body generally responds favorably to situations and options that result in the most dopamine being released into the brain.

Thus, making decisions becomes a process of choosing which option will give us the most rewarding experience or feeling. Since dopamine acts as a natural motivator, it helps motivate people to make decisions that may otherwise be difficult or produce an unfavorable outcome.

For example, someone who gets a dopamine rush from emotional eating might be motivated to reach for junk food whenever the stress hits. They will make this decision instantly without regard for future consequences. However, if they understand how dopamine influences their ability to make judgments, they may be more conscious of its effects and try to combat them. People can teach their brains to make wiser choices that will benefit them in the long run. Following are some steps to help people make good conscious decisions.

1. Visualize the future self, the successful self.

Imagery is a powerful technique for mental performance improvement. The technique is established on the assumption that, through visualization and repetition, an individual can create a mental representation of their actions alongside the physical ones in order to better adapt and respond in any given situation. Holmes and Collins (2001) found that visualizing success involves creating internal cognitive representations that mirror actual action. This helps release dopamine, improve motivation, and build confidence while encouraging improved execution when performing outside of one's imagination. As such, visualizing success can be an incredibly useful tool for any athlete or performer wishing to maximize their potential within a competitive environment.

Ever wondered what Olympic athletes are thinking just before they compete? Consider this: They're in front of thousands, if not millions, of people. They're apprehensive, monitoring their competition and thinking about everything that could go wrong and how to avoid it.

Doesn't that sound reasonable? After all, that's what any person would do in their situation. Well-trained athletes, on the other hand, understand that they should never visualize mistakes, especially shortly before a competition. Why? Because anticipating mistakes or poor performance increases the likelihood that the athletes will do those things during the event, even if they don't intend to.

Instead, many top athletes are taught to visualize their goals immediately prior to a competition. They see themselves winning the game, winning the race, or scoring the game-winning point. They are taught to "imagine" what they want to happen rather than what they don't want to occur. If they accomplish this, their chances of success skyrocket (Meyers and Schleser, 1980). Seeing themselves succeed helps people believe that they can.

Similarly, visualizing the ideal success provides a creative way to set achievable goals and be empowered to make smart decisions. Whenever we utilize visualization to reach peak performance, the brain produces dopamine and that actually motivates us to *be better*. We should start by writing down what success means to us. This is important because the definition of success differs widely across individuals.

For example, this could include financial independence, good health, supportive relationships, or anything else that motivates us. Then, find a relaxed position, close your eyes, and let your mind explore a daydream of what it is like to be that future version of yourself. Immerse yourself in the visualization exercise until you can really feel and experience what it is like to have achieved your desired success. Keep track of any inspirational moments in a journal or on paper so that they last forever. Creative visualization is an important practice, as it helps us determine which decision-making strategies will put us on track for achieving our goals and dreams.

Consider Alice's story. Alice was never one for daydreaming, but when she closes her eyes and tries to visualize the future self she wants to become, suddenly her imagination comes alive. She sees a version of herself that has achieved all of her wildest dreams and ambitions—she has started a successful business, traveled the world, and made meaningful connections with people everywhere.

Alice feels so inspired by this vision of herself that it fills her with energy and determination to pursue these goals more fiercely than ever before. So every morning, she takes some time out of her busy schedule to meditate on this visualization until it feels like reality in her mind. She begins to make diligent notes, create a mind map, fill her journal with things that ignite her inspiration, and decorate her little room with sticky notes.

Little by little, Alice begins making small changes that help lead her closer toward achieving what seemed impossible before. She takes online classes related to starting a business, makes new friends who share similar interests, saves money for travel—all actions that put into motion an unstoppable force toward progress.

So many people with so much wasted potential never see their dreams realized. They don't even believe in themselves to start with. This is why it's so important to visualize. It helps keep everything important in perspective.

Visualizing the future self is a great way to stay motivated and take action toward achieving long-term goals. It can be a mental image or even a description of how someone wants their life to look, down to the last detail. For example, they might imagine themselves five years in the future, living in a beautiful house of their own, working with their dream team at the office and enjoying an amazing view while having dinner with friends. Visualizing these things can create a subtle sense of hope and focus on what they want out of life. By setting small, tangible goals and putting markers along their path that signify progress and accomplishment, it's easier to stay on track even when times get tough. So chase those big dreams for the future self. Don't wait! Take some time today to start picturing what it will be like! And remember, when someone visualizes something, their brain interprets it as if it is truly occurring, which raises dopamine levels, thus boosting internal drive and motivation.

2. Personal perspective is key. The opinions of others are insignificant.

It's amazing how much of a difference a unique outlook on life can make to one's own mental state. Personal perspective is an important factor in helping people achieve greater levels of satisfaction. It might not seem like it, but modifying the lens with what we view a challenging situation can actually increase the production of dopamine in the brain. This is because the amount of dopamine released changes depending on how the action is perceived by the individual (McKeever, 2022). For example, someone who appreciates exercise will experience a two-times rise in dopamine, whilst someone who does not will not experience any. This implies that people have some control over how much dopamine their brain produces during an activity.

Their personal perspective and interpretation thus *color* their experience.

When people believe they are enjoying a challenge, they generate more dopamine, which stimulates and motivates them to do it again in the future. Considering this, it's no wonder that changing the mindset often brings about improvements in well-being, providing people with a new lease on positive energy that ultimately helps them make positive decisions!

While it is helpful to have an understanding of others' perspectives, relying solely upon other people's opinions to make decisions can become counterproductive. Taking into account the potential for varied advice and disagreements, ask those around what they think might cause further confusion. This confusion will lead to lower levels of self-confidence and self-worth, thus lowering the overall levels of dopamine as well. Lower levels of dopamine will lead to lower levels of motivation, and this will have an overtly negative impact on decision-making.

Therefore, before making any important decision, it is key to consider all the questions we need to ask ourselves in order to gain clarity and make an informed choice. It is important that we take the time for self-reflection so that we understand our own wants, needs, desires, and intentions. Having a clear understanding of what we want out of life will ensure that the decisions we make will better satisfy these goals.

Professor David Welch explains that people who don't take the time for self-reflection tend to make bad decisions because they do not understand their own position. He encourages readers to ask themselves specific questions like: "Will the outcome of my decision move me closer to what I truly want? Does the benefit outweigh the cost? Is the level of risk worth the reward? How committed am I to this change?"

These questions help individuals assess the situation and decide if a particular course of action is constricting in alignment with their goals. To further provide an example, Welch underscores how one should be sure they really want to marry somebody before taking such a huge step. Ask yourself: "Do I really want to marry this person, or do I just want to get married with kids someday?" "Will being with this person make me irrevocably happy?" We can have peace of mind in knowing our decision will bring satisfaction for years to come (consistently higher levels of dopamine) rather than regret soon after.

3. Align everything with core values, persevere, and fight on!

Having a purpose in life and aligning with one's core values can be extremely fulfilling. It gives people an underlying sense of purpose that is difficult to find elsewhere. Not only does this keep people motivated and satisfied, but it also makes them *happier*. This is backed up by science; when people are doing something meaningful, the brain releases dopamine. So if people want to increase their happiness and contentment levels, they should consider spending time on activities that are closely tied to their core values. Not only will this make them a more fulfilled individual, it'll also give their mind and soul a much needed boost!

Thus, aligning our lives with our core values is an important factor in achieving meaningful motivation. Before we decide on a course of action, it's important to take time to think about how it fits into our list of the highest-priority values, passions, and priorities that make up who we are. If there is a significant misalignment between the decision and our fundamental values, then chances are we won't find satisfaction regardless of the outcome. If something does not satisfy us innately or clashes with our core values, it's likely not going to bring us any joy, and that essentially means that no dopamine will be released as a result of participating in said activity.

Perseverance is the key to success in both sports and life. Whether it's someone who perseveres despite difficulties and setbacks or someone who tends to quit when faced with a challenge, they can still increase their ability to persevere with practice. Scientists have identified higher dopamine levels as being linked to forming habits like perseverance (Bergland, 2011). Dopamine is the fuel that helps motivate people to stay focused and work hard toward achieving their goals.

Everyone has heard the famous quote from Henry Ford, reminding us that work brings joy. But what does it mean when applied to perseverance? Quite simply, framing perseverance as an opportunity rather than a drudgery can actually boost neurochemistry, increasing confidence and well-being in the process. Rather than viewing the process of perseverance as a grueling, joyless experience, look at it through a different lens. When done this way, people will find that many elements of the journey become hedonic, helping them stay motivated and keeping them on track to achieve their goals.

By taking this mindset and making small changes to their perspective and attitude, they just might find themselves able to persevere with greater ease and satisfaction, all the while perfectly aligned with their inner selves. Neuroscientists have found that dopamine is connected to positive reinforcement, which means that when people make progress toward completing a task, such as studying for a test, their brain will produce more dopamine, giving them an inner feeling of satisfaction and increased striving power.

So if they want to strengthen their ability to stay on track despite adversity, they need to look for regular opportunities where they can observe small successes and let those accomplishments encourage more of the same!

To better understand themselves and succeed in making decisions based on their core values, create a list of what they are, and then evaluate how any prospective choice measures up against them before taking further steps toward putting it into action.

Having met a few individuals with an unwavering commitment to their goals, and often in awe of the way they carry themselves despite setbacks and failures, these "gritty" people possess a determination that enables them to persist and work hard toward achieving their vision. This quality is simply inspiring from afar and admirable when observed from up close. So before pursuing any dream or goal, it's important to have the inner fortitude needed to get there—something that can never be overlooked in anyone striving for success.

"Grit is passion and perseverance for very long-term goals. Grit is having stamina. Grit is sticking with your future, day in, day out, not

just for the week, not just for the month, but for years, and working really hard to make that future a reality. Grit is living life like it's a marathon, not a sprint." -Angela Lee Duckworth

Gusto, like grit, is an important characteristic of successful people. We must be passionate about the decisions we make in life. Passion has strength. So, when it comes to making the proper choice, we shouldn't fall back into our comfort zone and continue to work in a job we despise. Instead, find strategies to energize your soul and make huge strides toward your goals.

Setting and meeting deadlines is the key to successfully powering your dopamine production! We need to get into the habit of setting a timeline for ourselves, be it an hour or a week. An effective way to do this is to set up daily scheduling and goals—both big and small—that must be completed by our own individual deadlines. Additionally, use outside resources like timers, calendars, or even, dare we say, peer pressure. Enlist a partner with similar goals who can help with accountability and stick it out! At first, it may seem scary, but once we develop the habit of monitoring ourselves against a timeline, it will get easier day by day. And soon enough, we'll find ourselves becoming an efficient worker bee with a smooth dopamine flow too!

PART 2: DOPAMINE AND HABIT-FORMATION

When people engage in activities that produce rewarding experiences, their dopamine levels increase, creating a positive feedback loop where they're more likely to repeat the behavior because it is reinforcing. Over time, this cycle of getting rewarded for their behavior forms an automatic response—the beginnings of a habit. For example, someone who gets unbridled happiness (a rise in dopamine) from watching a romantic movie on the weekends will likely repeat that behavior because it is so innately satisfying. Over time, this occasional indulgence will turn into Friday movie nights with the girls and will etch itself into a routine. There is a direct relationship between how people feel when they perform a behavior and the likelihood of repeating the activity in the future.

Many seek out certain rituals or routines in order to create healthy habits, often believing that they are prescribed a certain number of days or hours needed to embody a particular habit. Contrary to popular belief, there is no concrete timeline, as every individual is unique and requires various amounts of time in order to embed a new behavior. In any circumstance, habit-forming relies heavily on the ability to *manipulate and exploit dopamine; in other words, it is how people feel about something, their emotions, that triggers the release of dopamine and dries behavioral change.* If something makes an individual feel incredibly alive and happy, chances are they'll ingrain that behavior into their routine.

Dopamine encompasses more than just short-term pleasure. Its capacity to dictate people's behaviors that form ingrained habits—such as brushing teeth or regularly exercising—is equally important for understanding human functioning. There is a direct relationship between how individuals feel when they perform a behavior and the probability of repeating the behavior in the future. If people have a strong, pleasant emotion associated with the new activity (higher levels of dopamine), habits can emerge rapidly, typically in just a few days (Fogg, 2019).

In fact, certain habits appear to be hardwired: individuals conduct the activity once and then don't examine other options again. You've established an instant habit. Consider giving a child a mobile phone; their emotional response to using the device can swiftly wire in a habit, and before the parents realize, the phone is connected to their hand.

In conclusion: *emotions create habits*. The way an individual feels about something determines whether or not they will repeat the same behavior in the future. The brain encodes the cause-and-effect link with the help of dopamine, which sets expectations for the future. People can circumvent this reward mechanism by inducing what neuroscientists call a "reward prediction error" in their brain.

The brain is constantly taking in the surrounding world and using this sensory input to make predictions about future experiences. When something happens that defies an individual's initial expectations, there is an adjustment process that occurs internally. This is known as a reward prediction error and results in dopamine being released, which allows them to then form new expectations of what might happen again in the future.

A great example of this could be when people try something that they think they won't like, but to their surprise, they end up loving it. This can happen with food, music, or any other experience; suddenly their expectations are updated based on this positive outcome that wasn't expected. Ever end up loving someone who absolutely did not make a good first impression? That is a great example of a reward-prediction error.

The brain is an amazing and intricate system that can be tapped into in order to gain a better sense of control over everything in life. Intentionally creating feelings has the potential to help people wire in the habits they wish to cultivate. By doing so, they are establishing signposts along ancient neural pathways, prompting their brains to relearn and change behaviors. This unlocks several opportunities, allowing them to modify their lives in more positive directions and access the remarkable power of human potential.

One of the reasons resolutions fail, diets fail, and resolve wanes is because maintaining motivation is difficult. That is not your fault. BJ Fogg, PhD, who founded the Behavior Design Lab at Stanford University, discusses this in his book *Tiny Habits: The Small Changes That Change Everything*. He shows people how to use his Tiny Habits method to hack their motivation and achieve lasting changes. It's simple: Break down major changes into small activities, locate where they naturally fit into everyone's life, and then celebrate. That's all.

Here's how we can make a habit take root in our brain quickly and easily:

1. Perform the behavior sequence and celebrate immediately afterward

Having a well-defined plan is an important factor in developing new habits and behaviors. By practicing the desired behavior sequence consistently, it becomes easier to incorporate into the daily routine, and the desired behavior becomes easier to do as well. The more people practice something, the easier it gets. That, in turn, lowers feelings of stress and frustration and raises overall satisfaction and happiness, meaning more dopamine to swim around!

For example, if someone wants to make reviewing their to-do list a part of their morning ritual, they can start by committing to turning on the coffeemaker as soon as they get up. Once that becomes second nature, they can add in getting out the to-do list right after.

Continue to repeat the sequence of behavior until it starts to feel as easy as breathing. If an our goal is to do some yoga in the morning, we can start off by taking an early shower and then practicing yoga afterward. We have to repeat this behavior for thirty minutes each day. It's important to celebrate right afterward. In fact, Fogg's research has shown that habits may emerge very fast, in just a few days, if people have a *strong, pleasant emotion* associated with the activity. Strong, pleasant emotions equal a strong presence of *dopamine in the brain*, and that in turn activates the positive feedback loop whereby the individual will keep on repeating said behavior due to the feeling of satisfaction attached with it.

As a result, it's critical that people rejoice soon after completing their new habit. "When you celebrate, you create a positive feeling inside yourself on-demand," explains Fogg. "This good feeling wires the new habit into your brain. When we feel good, our brain releases dopamine, we remember what behavior led to feeling good, and we're more likely to do it again."

When it is suggested that people should celebrate right after the conduct, take it very seriously. Immediacy is one factor that influences the rate at which people establish habits. The other factor is the strength of their emotions as they celebrate. The stronger the emotions, the more dopamine will be released.

This is a one-two punch: They must celebrate immediately following the conduct, and their celebration must feel genuine (intensity). The brain possesses a built-in system for encoding new habits, which they may circumvent by rejoicing. When they master the art of celebrating, they will have a superpower for forming habits. Before they know it, they'll have this healthy hack revitalizing their daily routine without requiring any extra time or effort expended.

Celebrating successes, large and small, can be the secret to incorporating positive habits into a person's life. This type of rewarding behavior has many advantages; it's free, fast, and accessible to everyone without prejudice. Not only that but learning how to treat ourselves kindly is one of the most beneficial abilities people can acquire. What better way to do this than to take time out of our day to acknowledge what we have achieved? Celebrations such as taking ourselves out for dinner or even just dedicating five minutes of peaceful reflection

are all excellent ways to reward good
behavior and create long-term positive
change.

Here are some ideas for celebrations.
Incorporate activities that can be done in the
middle of a crowd as well as in the seclusion
of home. Not all of the celebrations listed
here will be suitable for everyone. And that's
fine. Just choose whatever feels best.

With any accomplishment, it's important for
everyone to celebrate in their own unique
way. Whether we say "Yes!" or "Yay!" do a
fist pump, smile big, imagine a child clapping
for us, picture a crowd cheering, receive a
hug from a loved one, get ourselves a
chocolate or a bouquet, hum an upbeat song
we love—such as the theme from Rocky—or
even do a little dancy dance, they all make
great ways to recognize those successes and
remind ourselves of what we're capable of
achieving.

Clapping our hands, nodding our head, and
giving ourselves a thumbs-up are all simple
acts of self-acknowledgement that have the
power to turn any average day into a

celebration. Imagine the roar of a crowd cheering us on as we think to ourselves "Good job!" Take a deep breath and snap those fingers for added emphasis; after all, "you deserve it!" To take things up a notch, we can look up and make a V with our arms while smirking at ourselves in the mirror, proudly say out loud "I got this!" and imagine seeing fireworks surrounding and engulfing everything—just like any top-notch achievement should be celebrated!

Creating and reinforcing new habits has never been easier than with celebrations. Research has revealed that when people find a celebration that resonates with them and deliver it immediately after or while performing the action, their brain will develop the pathway to help make it an automatic behavior in the future.

Celebrations don't always have to be lavish events; they can be as simple or as extravagant as people desire them to be. It's important to identify a form of celebration that brings joy and encourages positive reinforcement for any successful actions taken moving forward, leading to healthier life choices and lasting habits.

2. Start Creating Micro Goals

Micro goals force us to break down our macro (or short-term and long-term) goals into manageable steps. They are particular action steps and task-oriented goals that will assist us in achieving our larger goals. They may appear like a to-do list.

Dopamine release after achieving even minor goals has been demonstrated to have a significant impact on behavior change and neuroplasticity. According to *Psychology Today*, making the bed and doing the dishes will give us the same *ding-ding-ding* sense of success. In terms of brain chemistry, the sense of accomplishment that follows the completion of a task functions as "rocket fuel," propelling us ahead toward our ultimate objective. But how can we create micro goals to garner that sense of accomplishment?

Begin by identifying long-term goals. To identify long-term goals, we need to ask ourselves a series of questions that relate to how a goal will contribute to having a more satisfying life. Questions like: "What makes me the happiest?" "What brings me the most meaning?" "What do I need to do to give myself and my life more meaning?" By considering these types of questions, we are clearer on what is in alignment with our values and can make an informed decision about which goal would support that alignment. Remember, when you align everything with your core values, you increase your life satisfaction and happiness; that means more dopamine!

Furthermore, this also helps us determine our "whys" as we continue to strive toward achieving our long-term goals. Knowing why we are choosing a particular goal keeps us motivated, inspired, and more likely to experience success.

Remember that everyone has a choice. No matter what goal we have chosen to pursue, reminding ourselves that we are in charge of the outcome can be immensely powerful. As opposed to viewing a task as an obligation, very simply repositioning this task and saying "I choose to do this" can give us back a sense of control and empowerment. For example, if a college student is feeling overwhelmed by class obligations, instead of feeling like he or she has no choice but to attend classes, simply shifting the language to "I choose to go to class" will help them create space for a sense of motivation and personal investment in their education.

Achieving each goal can seem daunting, but with a manageable plan to break down your goal into smaller achievable steps, it is much more attainable. Each step should be simple and should have its own specific date and time for completion. If this feels overwhelming, each step can be broken down even further to make sure the process is comfortable and attainable. This will also make it easier for people to hold themselves accountable for making progress with technology. With this actionable plan in place, they will be able to take small steps each day that lead to bigger successes as a whole.

For example, focusing on reading goals is tough, especially if someone is a beginner. But there's good news: It's totally achievable! If someone wants to read twelve books a year, all they need to do is commit to twenty pages a day. And if that strikes fear in their heart, don't worry; just focus on one page at a time. It might seem overwhelming, but when people slowly progress from page one . . . to page two . . . and then pick up the book afterward day after day, they'll be surprised how easily it goes! This strategy applies with every book; once one is finished, switch to the next. One page at a time, and before they know it, those twelve books will have been conquered.

PART 3: DOPAMINE AND PROCRASTINATION

While procrastination can have its benefits, it also can lead to an anxiety-ridden work environment and ultimately lower productivity. That pleasure we get when putting aside something difficult in exchange for short-term gratification is dictated by the release of dopamine in our brain. It's a signal that tells our body rewarding activities will follow, yet this pattern can easily become entrenched and create a cycle of procrastination that leaves us unsatisfied as tasks go unfinished or lag significantly behind deadline. Although dopamine may provide temporary comfort, if not managed properly, it can be detrimental to our work and leisurely tasks.

Delving into the neuropsychology of procrastination requires examining the complex interplay between both conscious and unconscious motivations. Neurophysiologically, procrastination is characterized by heightened activation in regions associated with risk-seeking behavior, motivational conflicts, goal-oriented behavior, and cognitive control (Svartdal et al., 2018). This suggests that decision-making under uncertain future risks involves increased engagement of regulatory processes that are impacted by a person's level of confidence in their ability to make a satisfying choice. Put simply, procrastination is often executed as an effort to control outcomes that could be perceived as threatening or aversive.

Procrastination can often impede an individual's path to success. While traditional wisdom might lead someone to believe that the underlying cause of procrastination is a time management problem rather than an emotional one, studies have suggested otherwise. According to Dr. Timothy Pychyl, a psychologist who specializes in procrastination, the only way to overcome this issue is by *evoking emotion*, rather than relying solely on logic and detached reasoning. His research suggests that we are more likely to put off tasks if decision-making is based on reason alone; instead, when we factor in our purpose behind wanting to take action and achieve our goal, we are less likely to be side-tracked by procrastination. Therefore, it's clear that when it comes to overcoming procrastination, emotion must be at the forefront of the thought process in order for us to truly make meaningful progress.

The limbic system is one of the brain's oldest and most powerful regions. It deals with emotions and memory, as well as regulating and influencing instinctive behavior caused by emotional inputs. This is where the amygdala is located. The amygdala plays an important role in how animals evaluate and respond to environmental risks and challenges, by assessing the emotional significance of sensory input and motivating an appropriate response. Its primary function is to regulate emotions such as fear and anger.

The prefrontal cortex is less developed and younger. It is where people actively prepare and make deliberate decisions. Since the limbic system is far more powerful, it frequently prevails when we are presented with a novel activity.

Automation outperforms conscious effort since it is built just for survival. The brain tries to protect the person from impending trauma. Most people are accustomed to avoiding unpleasant behaviors because of this. Although June ought to sit down and prepare that report, she puts it off since it makes her uncomfortable. Even though John should start working on his new idea, he puts it off because it requires him to enter uncharted terrain and stirs up unpleasant feelings of inadequacy and self-doubt. This is due to the fact that the amygdala governs our automatic emotional reaction to a scenario. The amygdala sets up a fight (resistance) or flight (neglect) response, and we immediately feel threatened by something as mundane as writing a report.

As psychotherapist Maribeth Arena bluntly elaborates, this emotional reaction is so fast, "It shuts down the logic part of our brain, and in 1/32 of a second, we become fearful and we can't think!"

As a result, we procrastinate: We postpone what we might and should have done today.

So why do we procrastinate? Because doing so is the quickest method to experience an immediate dopamine high. The limbic system pushes us to engage in activities that make us feel good right now. But what if people could control the quantity of dopamine produced by their body so that they have enough to keep them motivated and focused even when performing unpleasant tasks? Here are the best techniques to boost dopamine levels so everyone can fight procrastination and get things done.

How to Rewire the Brain and Stop Procrastinating

Procrastination can only be overcome emotionally, not rationally, because it is obvious that emotional problems rather than time management problems are its primary causes. Dr. Timothy Pychyl, a psychologist, says that "the more purpose we have, the less we procrastinate." This means that people are less likely to put off completing whatever task or goal they are working toward if they can identify the reasons *why they want to do it rather than just what they want to achieve.* This makes sense given the fact that people make decisions on the basis of their emotions in real life.

Challenges are a part of life, and in order to overcome them, all we need is to practice "tricking our brain." If we can turn challenging tasks into something that's exciting, we have more motivation to move forward. One way of achieving this is by using emotions and understanding the power behind them. For example, a traditional chain of thought might look like this: I need to do an hour of exercise today, but I'm lazy. I need to get done with this twelve-page report by tonight. I need to cook for my daughter's birthday. I need to clean my cat's litter box. (Brain: Procrastinate).

An emotional chain of thought might look like this: I need to do an hour of exercise today, but I'm lazy. (Brain: Procrastinate).You: But if I don't work out, that would make it almost a week without any movement! And then I'll get even lazier! I can't let that happen! And then I will start gaining a tremendous amount of weight! That'll make my PCOS worse! And then I will feel like absolute garbage! And then I will eat unhealthy food again! All the junk that I took years trying to give up! And then I will feel like garbage even more! And then I have to train ten times harder to get back into shape. Alrighty! ENOUGH! I'm going to the gym!

Second example: You, with an emotional chain of thought: If I don't get this done by tonight, I might fail this class! I will disappoint everyone I hold dear! This can't be happening! I shall power through even if it takes me all night!

It's so impressive that in both of these cases, the individual decided to pay attention to their emotions and take the time to explain to themselves why the fear of avoidance was greater than the fear of discomfort. They used this as a motivating factor and realized that not taking action was more terrifying than not doing what they said they would. As we all know, taking that first step toward a goal will always give us a hit of dopamine; if we just keep going and smashing out even more goals, it keeps on coming! But sometimes the amygdala takes over in a fraction of a second and puts the brakes on, leading people toward feeling scared or insecure about tackling something.

If we become aware of this and take a moment to consider why this work is important to us and what would happen if we don't do it, we may turn our limbic system's fear of avoidance against it and beat it at its own game.

Everyone knows that they should be doing the right things, but it's easy to forget why. Sometimes, the logic might make complete sense on a practical level but doesn't really move us into action. What spurs us into action is *acknowledging the implications of not doing what we should.* Does this really motivate us to take action? Are we aware of how it will affect us if we don't do what we need to do today? It might be beneficial to reflect on why and how it matters in order for us to act on our goals with passion and conviction.

The Three-Step Method to Rewire Our Brains and Stop Procrastinating

To successfully rewire the brain and move away from procrastination, *we must first get a crystal-clear understanding of why our goals even matter.* Dedicating a few moments to examining how we'd feel in the face of both inaction and action is important. Every individual's motivations are distinct, so taking the time to contemplate *how you specifically would be affected can help drive home the point of why it's important to take steps and complete your set goals.* This can also help provide guidance on how best to allocate resources, as well as serve as motivation during difficult stages.

Therefore, start by *creating a domino effect. Keep repeating one small action toward your goal to trigger a dopamine hit until the entire task is complete.* Taking small steps toward a goal can create a domino effect of positive reinforcement and help elevate motivation. Every time the task is completed, dopamine is released, creating a sense of drive and focus necessary to move on to the next step. Completing one task leads to another, and eventually the entire objective is achieved. This repeating cycle of incremental progress can be incredibly powerful in maintaining momentum and ensuring a successful final outcome.

Jane, for example, has to submit thirty thousand words within a two-week period. Looking at that final number alone would make most people pack their bags and leave. But Jane's different. She's strategic and will set a goal of writing three thousand words each day. This will give her all the necessary dopamine hits that she requires in order to boost her motivation and complete the task within the given time frame. Sometimes, however, self-doubt can derail Jane from meeting her deadlines, encouraging procrastination and overcomplicating things. But slowly and surely, she is learning that something is better than nothing and having written a few words is better than staring at a blank page. This alone motivates her into eventually finishing it.

It may seem daunting to take on a big goal, *so taking one small action toward that goal can be a great help.* Reaching milestones along the way can give us psychological motivation and the reward of dopamine hits, aiding in keeping our energy and enthusiasm up to reach our end goal. The range of small actions we take also helps keep us flexible along the way, as having an open mind for different options could create doors for inspiration, success, and growth. Small actions enable us to stay focused on what we are working toward while allowing us to measure our progress, ensuring eventual success with our goals.

Taking action is key to outsmarting procrastination. Step one is to understand the overall goal and why it's important to us; this will motivate us to act. Step two entails breaking down the goal into simple, manageable steps and taking those initial actions, no matter how small the action. This releases dopamine, which further motivates us because it feels good to take charge of something.

Lastly, step three requires sustained focus on one task at a time until completion; this reinforces why we must keep going despite any potential obstacles or roadblocks, as seeing the results of our hard work will bring satisfaction. By properly understanding each step, incorporating these steps into our daily life, and applying discipline when it comes to breaking down tasks, we are able to beat procrastination at its own game with ease.

PART 4: USING DOPAMINE TO IMPROVE DRIVE AND MOTIVATION

Aiden is languidly scrolling through his phone, and then suddenly, motivation hits him like a wave. He puts his phone down and gets to work. What is it about the moment that motivation kicks in that makes it so electric and transformative? The driving force behind our actions in response to our goals or anxieties is motivation. It is an outward driving force that compels us to act, originating from either internal or external stimuli.

The answer lies in the science of motivation and how our brain works. Through understanding the neuroscience behind this strong emotion, we can learn why this feeling has such an impact on us and how to use it to our advantage. There are several elements that make up the power of motivation, from dopamine incentives to activating neural patterns in the brain; understanding these basics will allow anyone to unlock their full potential for success.

Dopamine is responsible for motivation. The amygdala is a region of the brain in humans that plays a critical role in motivation. It responds to stimulation by sending a signal to the prefrontal cortex (PFC), which helps us comprehend information so we may either respond, ignore it, or store it in memory.

The brain makes notes when enjoyable things happen, such as eating cheesecake. The hippocampus is a structure in the brain that plays a pivotal role in learning and recovers our long-term memories in the future. It is what assists the brain and reminds it to increase dopamine levels and recover those tasty memories of the cheesecake we love.

Food rewards can also help us stay driven by reminding us of the delicious dopamine release we'll experience after the task is completed. In fact, Vanderbilt University researchers discovered that those who people perceive as "go-getters," or those who consistently exhibit motivation, had higher levels of dopamine signaling, which makes them more responsive to rewards.

When it comes to motivation, not only is dopamine released as part of the experience, but other brain elements are at work as well. According to research, our physiological state, surroundings, and past experiences all have an impact on our motivation (Simpson and Balsam). This involves several regions of the brain and is primarily governed by the amygdala. Even though these factors add to motivation, dopamine is critical in maintaining it. The dopamine signal travels between neurons and receptors within our brain synapses to maintain these connections. This also includes an extensive pathway known as the brain reward system or mesolimbic pathway, which leads into the cerebral cortex on the top of the brain.

The brain is always looking for ways to get more dopamine, and it knows how to do it! By triggering the move of dopamine through the reward system, the brain learns that a particular activity brings the person sweet pleasure. Think about it: when people work hard doing something they love, dopamine has a chance to flow through their brains and give them a pleasurable feeling. That feeling encourages people to keep going, because their brain knows that working on a particular thing brings rewards. When people start heading down that path of success, it's thanks in part to the way dopamine helps motivate them. This increases people's motivation in the long run.

There are tools that can help us use dopamine to motivate ourselves. These are divided into two parts:

Part I: Managing Dopamine to Sustain Motivation

People have a baseline level of dopamine, which can surge or drop depending on their behaviors, the substances they consume, or even their thoughts. Many things influence people's baseline dopamine levels, including genetics, behaviors, sleep, nutrition, and the amount of dopamine they experienced the previous day. It is crucial to maintain adequate amounts of baseline dopamine to sustain daily motivation. The baseline should neither be too low or too high. They can achieve a healthy baseline dopamine level by in the following ways.

Taking the time each morning to view early morning sunlight for a period of ten to thirty minutes can have powerful effects on the regulation of dopamine in the body (Cawley et al., 2013). Not only can it cause an immediate release of dopamine, but when practiced consistently, this activity may even lead to a rise in the expression levels of certain dopamine receptors. To maximize the benefits of this routine and add an extra layer of wellness, experts suggest taking a short cold shower—anywhere from one to three minutes in length—as cold as a person can reasonably tolerate. Research has shown that this simple addition can drastically raise people's baseline dopamine level for multiple hours afterward.

Appropriate sleep helps regulate the production and release of dopamine, resulting in better brain functioning (Julson, 2022). To make sure the body gets the rest it needs, aim for seven to eight hours of quality sleep through the night, preferably without any sleep-inducing drugs. Try to incorporate natural ways to aid falling asleep, such as dimming the lights after dark, putting on a humidifier, playing soft music, and spraying a lavender scent on the pillows. Additionally, avoid caffeine or sugary foods near bedtime, as these can disrupt hormones associated with dopamine. Finally, follow a routine for going to bed and waking up, as this can help regulate the body's hormonal patterns and improve dopamine balance.

Exposing the eyes to bright lights during the late evening and early morning can cause serious sleep disruption (Suni, 2022). Research has discovered a direct link between bright lights at night and reduced dopamine levels, connected to the activation of the habenula (an emotion center responsible for controlling a wide range of emotion-related behaviors such as anxiety, fear, reward, and depression) in the brain. While occasional exposure won't have an extended long-term impact, the best way to keep a healthy sleeping pattern is to stick to dim lighting during these hours. If anyone is struggling with their circadian rhythms due to shift work or jet lag, it's helpful for health to take heed of this advice. Turn off all bright lights as soon as the sun starts to set.

Caffeine can be a great way to boost your energy levels and productivity throughout the day. Ingesting around one hundred to four hundred milligrams of caffeine per day, in whatever form is most feasible—coffee, tea, or perhaps even a tablet—can induce a mild increase in dopamine activity in the brain. Simultaneously, **this will also cause an increase in dopamine receptors**, which makes the body more sensitive to naturally occurring dopamine. It's important to limit caffeine intake prior to sleeping since its effects can remain active for up to six hours. To get the optimal benefit from caffeine use without disrupting sleep patterns, it's thus best to avoid consuming it after 2 p.m., with only rare occasions as exceptions.

Part II: Managing Dopamine Peaks

A dopamine peak is a release of dopamine when an individual undergoes a highly pleasurable experience. People often experience dopamine peaks when they do something they enjoy or when they reach an important goal. It can be triggered by anything from eating chocolate cake to passing an exam, or just any moment of pure happiness! Frequent dopamine peaks can help boost mood, creativity, and memory formation, but managing these dopamine peaks is critical for continued success.

Without a plan, the dopamine people get from small wins and goals will quickly diminish, leaving them feeling less energized and motivated in the long run. To get the most out of that powerful dopamine reservoir, it's important to leverage its effects to increase motivation and drive. Keep track of small wins and set aside special rewards for reaching milestones. By managing those dopamine peaks, people can stay on course for success and not get desensitized.

Here's how we can use the power of dopamine released by attaining milestones to boost long-term motivation.

Random Intermittent Reward Timing (RIRT)

If someone wants to stay motivated and have success in whatever pursuits they have, random intermittent reward timing (RIRT) could be their ticket. Casinos use this technique to take people's money because it works one hundred percent of the time, but that doesn't mean it has to be used against anyone! It can actually be applied to their favor by helping them stay motivated and stand strong when challenges arise.

To use RIRT, celebrate successes or milestones occasionally but not all of the time; we ought to mix in times when we just keep going and winning without an expectation of a reward. This will help us associate winning with the effort with the process itself; this is the holy grail of dopamine management. It won't make anyone dull or sad; it will make everything easier and more joyful. Without the dopamine peaks and valleys that external-reward-driven people suffer, we will be receiving all the external rewards anyway, just not as frequently as someone who's not using RITI.

For example, we could reward ourselves every time we complete a big project. We don't have to celebrate all the milestones leading up to the final work. We could celebrate maybe some, but not all. These intermittent rewards will ignite intrinsic motivation and passion within us, and before we know it; we'll be doing whatever we are doing for the effort of the process itself and not some expectation of reward.

Remembering that dopamine is subjective is essential to staying motivated and tracking progress. The brain generates more dopamine when an event's association with internal chemical releases (like dopamine) is known. This means understanding how much executive control the prefrontal cortex has over the subjective feeling of motivation and direction toward a goal is critical. It is even possible for us to tell ourselves that we can reach our personal goals, and this helps trigger dopamine release. Doing so significantly gives us a mental boost in the right direction, though lying to ourselves about winning when we have in fact lost does not help at all. We must be honest with ourselves about what we actually have or have not accomplished in order to make real strides toward achieving our desired outcomes.

People are sometimes easily distracted during periods of goal work. But, Dr. Emily Balcetis, a professor of psychology at NYU, suggests a technique that's simple and effective: **spotlighting. It involves focusing one's visual attention on one specific point in the distance, which helps to reduce distractions.** That little reprieve from doing something monotonous can give the brain a dopamine boost, improving concentration and clarity. For example, sitting and reading or typing for hours continuously can be really draining and boring. Consider setting the book or laptop aside and focusing on something in the distance (could be anything, a chair, a table, a painting, a poster, etc.). This change is exciting for the brain, and it releases dopamine, thinking, "Oh, oh! We're done!"

Spotlighting helps to maintain focus but also encourages the release of dopamine and other neurochemicals, which puts us in a state of readiness and clarity. When we physically focus our visual attention on a specific point in the distance, it not only increases motivation due to the improved clarity it provides, but encourages the release of dopamine and other regulatory neurochemicals.

This is particularly useful when attempting tasks that require sustained effort or focus, as it has been shown to impact our brain's ability to stay engaged in activities for longer periods. Spotlighting seems like an easy tool to help us stay efficient and focused, especially during times when our attention span might otherwise wander.

Making strategic use of dopamine sources can help people reach their goals. **However, it is important to be mindful that stacking these sources of dopamine can have a detrimental impact on our long-term motivation, leading to powerful post-workout crashes.** As an alternative approach, we can try allotting ourselves the same amount of time and energy for workouts, but varying the source of dopamine.

For instance, when working out, we could try one session with caffeine or energy drinks, one session with music or friends/social connections, and one without any instant gratification triggers at all. By changing up our approach in this way, not only do we benefit from the stimulating nature of dopamine downers and enhanced engagement and drive, but we also build up motivation and resilience to potential fatigue by helping ourselves focus on more sustainable sources of inspiration.

Understanding and sustaining the dopamine baseline, as well as what spikes dopamine, will allow us to learn to regulate ours for long-term goal-directed motivation. We don't have to accomplish everything on the list; it's designed to be a sampling of possibilities. Use all or some as needed.

PART 5: DOPAMINE AND THE GROWTH MINDSET

The "Growth Mindset," a concept developed by Stanford psychologist Carol Dweck, is predicated on the idea of deriving pleasure from putting in effort toward achieving one's goals. Growth-minded individuals don't measure their success with the outcome, but rather based on how much effort they are able to put forth. In addition to greater internal validation and resilience, this approach to goal setting can create a source of sustainable motivation. Studies have also associated growth mindsets with higher performance levels, increased capacity for risk taking, lower stress levels, and better relationships at work. This can be understood more when people look at it through an understanding of dopamine and its biological effects.

Not only do those with a growth mindset have an improved ability to reach their goals, but they also experience pleasure during the journey. This is because dopamine is released in response to the effortful activities that are integral to success. The science behind this lies in the brain, specifically the mesolimbic pathway in the prefrontal cortex that allows people to train their cognition to find pleasure in challenging situations. For those looking to cultivate a growth mindset, reframing self-talk is paramount when facing difficulty on the path toward achieving their goal.

Adopting an empowering mindset can be a valuable tool in achieving great things. By telling ourselves "the difficulty I'm experiencing is a signal that I'm moving toward my goal," we spark the necessary motivation to keep striving forward despite any challenges. This acknowledgement of progress brings satisfaction and, with time and effort, inevitably rewards. It's an incredible shift in the way everyone perceives hard work; instead of dreading it, people begin to crave the challenge and feel accomplished upon making further strides along their journey. Everyone needs encouragement at times, so by using positive language like this as a reminder of our own strength, we can take back control and take ownership of our accomplishments.

The capacity to gain mastery of our senses lies within the realm of possibilities thanks to the wonders of the human brain. The mesolimbic pathway in the prefrontal cortex allows us to essentially "rewire" how we process stimuli, thereby transforming a difficult task into one that is far more pleasurable and enjoyable. By controlling the dialogue we direct toward ourselves during challenging moments, it is possible to plant the seeds for cultivating a growth mindset. Certainly, those who have been able to re-train their brains so they can release dopamine while going through limitations have unlocked a superpower most others only dream of possessing.

Practical Steps to Develop a Growth Mindset

1. First, the individual must believe they can do it.
Developing a growth mindset requires believing in our own power to succeed. One way to ensure this is to create a daily mantra

to remind ourselves of this fact. Regular repetition of this statement will help us reach and maintain the faith in ourselves and our abilities that will be essential for manifesting change. It might take some effort, but if we keep the end goal of growth and success in mind, we'll find that the repeated affirmation can do wonders for our self-confidence.

People need to understand that there is a lot of power in having faith in ourselves and believing that we can control our reactions. Self-belief and confidence are the driving force behind regulating dopamine because it gives us the drive to live life without feeling overwhelmed by our emotions or environment. Without confidence in ourselves, regulating dopamine becomes much more difficult. It's not impossible, though; it just takes regularly reinforcing what we believe in and centering our thoughts on achieving balance with dopamine levels.

2. Avoid blaming circumstances or others for their shortcomings.

If we find ourselves unable to achieve our goals, it's important to be honest about the cause and avoid placing blame on external circumstances or other individuals. Owning up to our mistakes and taking responsibility for learning from them is the key to achieving success in the long run. Reframing any negative situation at hand as an opportunity to learn will enable us to move forward in a productive manner and develop better practices for future success.

Productivity leads to confidence, and confidence leads to the release of dopamine. We ought to carefully analyze a situation and make sure that whatever occurred wasn't due to our own shortcomings or oversights. For example, someone not scoring enough points in an exam might feel the need to blame the college or their teacher. Doing so would make them overlook their own weaknesses, and thus their life would hardly ever improve. On the other hand, if they turn this situation around and work hard and succeed, they will also gain confidence and feel joy along the way. Therefore, successfully regulating their dopamine.

3. Those seeking change must also be curious.

Curiosity is such an innate part of being human, and interestingly enough, its stimulation is known to trigger the release of dopamine in the brain. Dopamine is a neurotransmitter that communicates messages between nerve cells and helps to regulate emotion, motivation, and pleasure. So when we are fascinated by something, this unregulated emotion is rewarded with the release of dopamine. Learning more about things we are curious about can be quite rewarding in terms of our health, as it boosts motivation and encourages us to learn more!

The world is full of possibilities to explore, grow, and learn; it's so easy to forget just how much there is out there. Whether we are seeking to drive change in the world or make a difference in our own life, curiosity is essential. When we question the unknown and dig further into topics that interest us, we open a door to connecting with others, understanding multiple perspectives, and seeing complex problems in new ways.

Being curious means allowing ourselves to let go of what we think we know (or don't) and actively seek knowledge that can help push our goals forward. It's those who ask questions, take risks, and continue searching for answers who will create real change over time.

4. Allow failure to occur.

Stories of grand successes and humble beginnings abound but often fail to consider the potential failures that come before that success. The reality is, failure can be a far more valuable lesson. When we allow ourselves to fail, that requires bravery and courage. Not only that, but it means learning from our mistakes in order to move forward and avoid repeating them again. It takes resilience, strength, and a lot of persistence; nothing great was ever achieved without it. So we shouldn't get down on ourselves when things don't go as planned; use those experiences to do better next time.

Allowing failure to be a part of life is a surprisingly powerful tool in maintaining mental and emotional well-being. It provides an incentive to keep going no matter how many obstacles appear in our path, because if nothing else, it can spark a neurotransmitter response that encourages us to keep at it. That neurotransmitter is dopamine, released every time we experience success but also when we endure a setback. Feelings of bravery, resilience, and strength all boost confidence and instill hope. Dopamine thrives on these and allows us to further improve and grow.

This offers an opportunity to learn from our mistakes and find new creative solutions while still feeling positive due to the dopamine boost.

5. Leave the comfort zone and become at home operating outside it.

Leaving the comfort zone can be scary, sure, but it's where the real magic happens. Think of stepping outside it as expanding the horizons; trying something new or pushing up against perceived limits could ultimately bring about a whole new level of self-actualization. Being able to welcome unfamiliar territory as a challenge and embrace it will open so many doors for personal growth. Growing through discomfort will no doubt stretch us in ways we never expected, so why not give it a go? Remember, dopamine is released every time we do something novel and resourceful, so get going!

PART 6. Don't place undue emphasis on results.

Self-gratitude for simply trying something can keep our motivation strong over the long run and help us get through those tough times. Always remember it isn't always about the destination; sometimes, it's about enjoying the journey! All great things began with an idea, and the ideas themselves were what paved the way for all the dreams mankind has accomplished till now. So, what is it exactly that keeps us going despite risk of failure? Dopamine! The spark of an idea itself generates copious amounts of dopamine that propels us to take further action. For example, a writer can celebrate after having finished a chapter. The rush of dopamine will encourage them to pursue finishing the book. If they focus on just the final result, they will never be able to enjoy the time spent actually writing the book.

They will get discouraged and demotivated when faced with hurdles.

One of the most rewarding journeys anyone can take is the pursuit of personal growth. Every day, we take small steps toward achieving a better version of ourselves, and as each new milestone is reached, a dose of dopamine is produced as a reward for each effort made. This process is essential for encouraging us to continue on our journey, allowing us to embark upon new paths and explore undiscovered territories whenever we desire. The act of striving never stops, but by taking pride in all the small steps that generate dopamine along the way, the magnitude of both success and happiness can be greatly increased.

It's easy to put all the focus on the end result and forget that getting there is just as important. Celebrate each small victory no matter how minuscule it may seem; those small wins add up! Whether it's finally finishing a chapter of a book or learning something complicated, make sure the importance of effort when working toward reaching any goal is not overlooked.

PART 7. Be aware of the green-eyed monster: envy.

Don't let envy creep into life. Sure, it can sometimes seem like someone else has all the luck when they get an amazing opportunity or achieve great success; don't let that be what life is all about! Instead, use it as motivation and capitalize on the inspiration. We should make that success something to reach for in our own life, rather than feeling weighed down by anyone else's experience. Jealousy should not be driving anyone to do great things. Envy just dulls that spark of ambition and makes it hard to keep going; don't get lured in by the green-eyed monster!

Envious people are more likely to be unfriendly, resentful, furious, and irritated. Such people are also less inclined to be grateful for their excellent characteristics and circumstances. Envy is linked to sadness, anxiety, bias formation, and personal misery. Everything that dopamine is not!

8. Lastly, don't let the protection of the ego get between the changes that could make you happier and more successful.

Protecting the ego can feel like the safest option, but it's not the route to success. Concentrating on progress rather than perfection is integral for developing a successful and healthy mindset. Focusing on effort over outcome allows one to remain engaged in their pursuits, instead of getting discouraged by past mistakes and failures. To succeed, it is important to be willing to learn from mistakes, push boundaries, and accept that even if it feels incredible and amazing right now because of accomplishing something great, there are always higher levels one can reach.

It is important to remember that we can only improve with the help of constructive criticism and feedback. If we allow their egos to impede this process, we are hindering our own potential for greater success and happiness. Letting go of our need for self-protection can open up an entirely new realm of growth and achievement; changing our perspective can revolutionize our life! Therefore, think positively and see every hindrance or challenge as simply what it is— a challenge that will eventually be defeated.

PART 6: DOPAMINE AND SELF-CONTROL

Instant gratification, also known as immediate gratification, is the desire to satisfy a craving immediately without regard for the long-term consequences or the wider picture. For example, the desire to have a high-calorie treat rather than a health-promoting snack, or the desire to use the snooze button rather than getting up early to exercise. The fact is, most people would rather get their instant dopamine fix than practice any form of self-control when faced with cravings. Self-control involves doing things without expecting an instant reward (a dopamine rush). Most people are uncomfortable with feelings of anxiety that result from letting go of instant pleasures.

Doing things like exercising, learning a new skill or language, working toward a goal, or taking time to meditate can build up our baseline dopamine level over time and make us more motivated and focused. The key difference being that we must delay gratification in order to experience success; by doing this, the reward centers are engaged, contributing to better focus and resourcefulness long term.

Self-discipline can be incredibly powerful in amplifying the positive moments that we experience in life. When more disciplined, we don't miss out on pleasure and satisfaction by dulling our senses with less-than-ideal activities or substances. Instead, the paradox of pleasure is that those energetic highs come not from chasing after pleasure but from actively shunning it; living our life with purpose and seeing results develop accordingly, we will feel more dopaminergic joy than having fleeting momentary gratification.

Everyone has goals, and striving to reach them is ultimately what drives us to be the best versions of ourselves over time; without self-discipline, we simply wouldn't gain enough momentum to get there. Making changes is an important part of life, but it can be difficult to stop from reverting to old habits and routines. Luckily, a few key practices, such as self-control and willpower, can help improve anyone's quality of life both mentally and physically. This has been scientifically proven by a team led by Dr. Pino, who found that dopamine levels play a significant role in the ability to maintain focus and resist impulsive behaviors. He postulates that "dopamine plays a wide role in the brain, from movement to cognition. Lowering dopamine levels may be able to reduce impulsivity, but we need to be certain that this didn't come at the expense of other, important functions."

The results of the study, published in the *Journal of Neuroscience* and led by Professor Ray Dolan, revealed a remarkable connection between dopamine levels in the brain and an inclination toward immediate gratification. Dopamine, known to be crucial for reward comprehension, pleasure, and memory formation via reinforcement, plays a key role in decision-making. People suffering from attention deficit/hyperactivity disorder (ADHD), characterized by elevated levels of dopamine production, often exhibit impulsive behavior, and this research provides valuable insight as to why that may be the case.

Douglas Lisle's TEDx talk aptly demonstrates the challenge of effectively navigating pleasure traps. This is exemplified by his description of an experiment involving a caged bird who had access to a button that released cocaine in its brain. Despite being provided with food, water, and mating opportunities nearby, the bird chose to relentlessly press the button until its eventual death two weeks later. During this process, it had neglected other activities essential for its survival and well-being. This vivid example serves as an important reminder of how our brain's reward system can lead us down paths not necessarily aligned with our best welfare and long-term success.

Making conscious choices that increase the dopamine baseline is the first step toward breaking this vicious cycle. Refraining from quick hits and instead focusing on activities such as physical exercise, learning, working on long-term goals, and meditation can have a direct impact on our motivation levels and our ability to focus. This is because dopamine helps us stay motivated when seeking a reward, even if it takes time before we receive it. With increased doses of natural dopamine from these healthy activities, we can become less dependent on triggers for stimulation, creating pathways for improved mental health.

People experience more fulfillment and pleasure since they are not desensitizing themselves by practicing self-discipline and regulating their dopamine. The paradox of pleasure is that *if we seek it, we will lose it; if we abandon it, it will follow us like a shadow.* Therefore, self-control is an important skill to master if we want to stay productive. One effective way of strengthening our self-control is to practice voluntary discomfort. This means deliberately subjecting ourselves to uncomfortable situations and avoiding the urge to give in easily to the comfort we could derive from easier solutions.

Voluntary discomfort mostly refers to physical pain, such as sitting for a longer period of time or going for a long run; anything that tests our ability to persevere and carry out difficult tasks with resolve instead of giving in quickly. This ancient Stoic exercise was first recorded by Seneca in his Moral Letters to Lucilius over two thousand years ago, suggesting it is highly effective when used consistently. Voluntary discomfort can ultimately help us strengthen our willpower and build self-discipline so that we can achieve more of what we desire in life.

"Set aside a certain number of days, during which you shall be content with the scantiest and cheapest fare, with course and rough dress, saying to yourself the while: 'Is this the condition that I feared?'" -Seneca

There are two main forms of voluntary discomfort: get uncomfortable and forgo pleasure.
Get Uncomfortable and Forgo Pleasure

Getting uncomfortable might not seem like a desirable task, but it actually has quite a few benefits. For example, when we sleep without a comfortable mattress or take cold showers, our body is pushed to become stronger and more adaptable. We can also save money on our utility bills by forgoing the AC/Heater or eating very simple meals. Of course, as with any habit, there's an element of discipline involved; if we're used to having all the comforts of home, it's understandable if taking cold showers isn't our first instinct! Despite this initial reluctance, however, we may find ourselves surprised at how well our body adjusts to the challenge and begins reaping the rewards—both physically and mentally—of learning how to get comfortable with discomfort.

It could be as simple as not scratching an itch on our body to engage in spontaneous voluntary discomfort. It is entirely up to us on how we wish to participate in becoming uncomfortable, but the key thing to remember is that once we've decided to do it, we should never back out. If we choose to sleep on the floor for the night, we don't get to get back up in the middle of the night and go back to bed, and we can't give ourselves an excuse to stop.

The first step is to recognize how the pursuit of pleasure can trap us in a condition of unhappiness. If we want something, we use the following formula:

Me + X = Bliss

The X can be anything: a new car, a home, the ability to accomplish a difficult yoga position.

The possibilities are unlimited. Obtaining the X will frequently result in a momentary feeling of satisfaction, but it will be replaced by another X (when we obtain that one, we will be truly pleased!). The "M + X" formula reinforces the sense that we are incomplete, that something is missing.

This sense of inadequacy causes a state of continual restlessness, or in certain circumstances, significant sadness ("if only I had a sexier body," "if only I were richer," "if only I had studied something rather than veterinary science in college"). That last one requires obtaining a time machine, which is doubtful, so the feeling of incompleteness is difficult to overcome.

We need to start by taking some time to consider the Xs (not romantic ones) in our life, write them down, and consider how they make us feel. Consider occasions in our life when we got what we really desired. Did it bring us lasting enjoyment, or did we merely add another X to our list?

Realizing that pursuing pleasure does not lead to long-term satisfaction is not bad news; in fact, it is quite freeing to realize that life does not have to be a never-ending quest. Dropping the "M + X" mentality and accepting that we are already complete is not the same as giving up doing fun things to improve our health and well-being—quite the contrary. Genuine self-improvement comes from a position of self-love, not a guilty sense of not being good enough. When we are happy with ourselves and truly value ourselves, we will automatically do what is best for us, doing it for the purpose of doing it rather than for some future reward.

That's what they mean by "living in the now" and "forgoing pleasure!" People start doing things not for some ultimate reward, but simply because they *want to*.

Writing it down before we begin can help us combat the possibility of quitting. For instance, write somewhere that "I will not give up sleeping on the floor tonight no matter how unpleasant it becomes" or "I know I can do this, even if my body is telling me that I can't."

Forgoing pleasure in the twenty-first century might seem easy at first glance, but in reality, it is more difficult than getting uncomfortable. To do so today would mean forgoing coffee or alcohol, desserts or snacking, social media, streaming platforms like YouTube or Netflix, as well as games. This includes a range of activities that have become incredibly popular in recent years and surpasses what was expected during 40 AD Rome when this exercise originated. Thus, engaging in this is difficult due to its complexity and requires immense dedication to be successful living without all these comforts and pleasures.

Cutting the plush entertaining comforts of modern life often reveals people's true capacity for endurance and resilience. For those brave enough to take up this challenge, enduring the hunger associated with intermittent fasting becomes much simpler when the typical forms of entertainment are removed. This is because their primary purpose is distraction—both from reality and from even more meaningful activities that could greatly benefit their overall well-being.

So instead of spending inordinate amounts of time on unfulfilling activities like scrolling through social media, why not partake in some voluntary discomfort and eliminate these distracting factors entirely? Doing so allows us to open ourselves up to a surprising level of inner resolve and strength, allowing us to better navigate through hardships as we progress through life. Forgoing pleasure can be a creative and highly effective way to practice voluntary discomfort.

The best way to go about it is by committing to it for a set number of days, giving ourselves parameters that are achievable but still difficult enough. To ensure you stick with it, write down the rules beforehand and make it as specific as possible; for instance, "I will abstain from all forms of modern entertainment, such as social media and streaming services, for three days." If you want to maximize the benefits of voluntary discomfort through the act of forgoing pleasure, combine it with other challenges, such as getting uncomfortable and pushing your limits even further.

PART 7: NOVELTY AND DOPAMINE

While most people typically think of dopamine as a reward-system chemical within the brain, it can also promote healthy thinking habits. By understanding how dopamine is connected to experiences that involve novelty, it is possible to encourage positive mental habits. Many interesting experiences are accompanied by positive psychological effects due to the role dopamine plays in anticipating and experiencing the unfamiliar. Therefore, making an effort to step out of your comfort zone by seeking out new and different activities may be very beneficial in developing strong thinking habits.

New and exciting experiences, when thoughtfully explored and discussed, can significantly enhance cognitive functions. Since learning new things is often a source of excitement for people, the excitement causes a rush of dopamine. Thus, novelty activates the dopamine system, which is directly responsible for learning. Here's an example:

Ever thought about why video games are so addictive? While playing and reaching a new level or world, it's almost impossible to resist the urge to keep going! That's because the brain actually encourages people to explore and seek rewards when exposed to something new. Recent studies on animals have shown that when their brain senses something new, dopamine levels rise! This dopamine then drives them to want rewards, and seeking them out creates an even bigger dopamine release. So if someone can't resist diving into a new game or exploring a place unknown, it's probably because their brain is driving them with wants of discovery and reward!

The hippocampus, a seahorse-shaped brain area, encodes information about people's everyday experiences, such as where and when an incident occurred. If something new catches their attention, they're more likely to remember what happened just before or after the event. Dopamine-releasing neurons project into the hippocampus from two brain regions: the locus coeruleus and the ventral tegmental area. Dr. Robert W. Greene of the University of Texas Southwestern Medical Center and Dr. Richard G.M. Morris of the University of Edinburgh led a team of researchers to study whether dopamine cells in either of these brain regions are involved in novelty-induced memory enhancement in mice. The findings implied that dopamine produced by neurons in the locus coeruleus is responsible for novelty-induced memory improvement.

Improving the way we learn is an important part of building our knowledge base. Adding something new to the way we learn can help our brain remember more effectively and allow concepts to stick with greater ease. This could be as simple as changing up our learning environment or using a variety of methods, such as visual aids, notetaking, and verbal repetition. It can also incorporate study skills techniques, such as breaking down material into smaller chunks or creating study aids that highlight key points. Being creative with how we learn allows us to make learning fun and engaging, boosting memory retention and helping new ideas become permanent fixtures in our mind. Following are some methods to naturally increase dopamine when trying to successfully learn something.

A great way to solidify previously acquired knowledge is to constantly add new information whenever revisiting the subject. This allows the brain to make better use of familiar content, as the stimulation of novel concepts can help emphasize more thoroughly understood concepts. The mixture of well-known information with fresh material helps create a strong connection between old and new ideas, which can be especially beneficial for further learning endeavors. For example, doctors have to constantly keep updating and adding new things to their already acquired pool of knowledge. One reason for this is that the world of medicine is technologically advancing each day, and they need to keep themselves updated, but it also helps them connect ideas and polish off old concepts.

The conditions of the environment can have far-reaching effects on the ability to comprehend and understand material. **By making subtle changes to the atmosphere** in which we are learning, it is possible to stimulate new connections in the brain. Such changes may include consuming content with an altered tone of voice, rearranging furniture, and adjusting the temperature or lighting in the room. A slight variation in any number of these elements can impact cognition, leading to greater understanding and more enjoyable learning experiences.

Remember, that new experiences are key to promoting cognitive function. Through embracing new opportunities, we can stimulate the release of feel-good chemicals and continuously acquire fresh knowledge that helps to challenge our brain and push us into new directions. Experiencing things differently (even a subtle change such as changing the lighting or rearranging the furniture) provides diverse experiences that allow us to develop our skill sets further. Whether it's trying a new cultural cuisine or exploring the city, by having unique experiences, we're able to broaden our thinking and boost problem-solving capabilities.

Moreover, when in novel situations, we often make decisions based on more information than usual, allowing us to come up with creative solutions (such as overcoming challenges in video games). With this variety of stimulation from different backgrounds, we can truly reach our intellectual potential by constantly learning something new.

Learning immediately after engaging in new experiences capitalizes on our brain's inherent plasticity—its capacity for adaptation and modification. This neurobiological phenomenon can be heuristic for learning, enabling people to learn more quickly. When it comes to setting aside time for studying, consider the opportunities presented by the unfamiliar—for example, scheduling a coffee chat with someone outside of your circle or undertaking a weekend trip to a different city. By taking advantage of novel stimuli, we can effectively exploit our cognitive capacities.

Chapter Takeaways:

- When we do something entertaining, such as watch a comedy, our brain produces dopamine, which makes us feel good. The brain then recalls how pleasant this experience was and seeks it out again in the future. Thus, dopamine is responsible for motivating us to repeat rewarding actions or activities.

- When making a major decision, feel free to employ both hemispheres of the brain (instead of just the logical left side). It is critical to strike a balance between emotion and logic. A great example is listening to relaxing music in order to stimulate both sides of the brain whilst faced with a problem or writing something.
- There is a direct link between how we feel when we execute a behavior and our likelihood of repeating the activity in the future. If we have a strong positive emotion linked with the new action, habits can form quickly, usually within a few days.
- That pleasure we get when putting aside something difficult in exchange for short-term gratification is dictated by the release of dopamine in our brain. It's a signal that tells our body rewarding activities will follow.
- Those with a growth mindset have an improved ability to reach their goals, but they also experience pleasure during the journey. This is because

dopamine is released in response to the effortful activities that are integral to success.

- Self-discipline can be incredibly powerful in amplifying the positive moments that we experience in life. When more disciplined, we don't miss out on pleasure and satisfaction by dulling our senses with less-than-ideal activities or substances.

- When we are introduced to something new, our brain really motivates us to explore and look for rewards. Recent animal experiments have demonstrated that dopamine levels increase when the brain detects something novel. They get motivated to seek out prizes as a result of this dopamine, which causes an even greater dopamine release.

CHAPTER 4: DOPAMINE AND GAMIFICATION

The addictive nature of many apps, from fitness to language-learning, can be attributed to a principle known as gamification. Within the context of gamification, game elements such as levels, points, deadlines, and rewards are offered in place of real-world incentives. This motivates users to use an application or service more frequently. Despite its complex meaning, gamification essentially boils down to one phenomenon: pleasure. Whenever people overcome an obstacle on their app of choice, whether that's a difficult word puzzle or a tough workout goal, the part of their brain responsible for reward and motivation is activated, providing them with a brief yet rewarding dopamine rush. Thus, apps that effectively employ game elements become markedly enjoyable over time and consequently dominate their markets.

So what exactly is gamification? It is the process of incorporating game mechanics into non-game activities. A game-like design contributes to the entertainment and engagement of information and goods. Gamification solutions can be used for everything from employee training to client loyalty programs.

Gamification has become an incredibly popular tool for increasing user engagement and driving motivation, particularly in non-game contexts. At its core, the technique works by introducing elements found in video games into a task, such as rewards and competition, while also encouraging social connectivity with other users.

This strategy has proven to be very successful when implemented correctly; many businesses are leveraging gamification to engage their customers more effectively and enhance user experience. A great example of this is "Zombies, Run!" an app that has been widely praised for its innovative way of turning exercise into an enjoyable gaming journey that allows users to interact with each other. Ten years since it was first released, this groundbreaking app continues to be highly successful in motivating people to reach their physical fitness goals.

Dopamine is stimulated anytime people achieve anything positive, and is responsible for how well games operate. It is, in essence, the medicine that makes them feel wonderful. When people play video games like *Super Mario Bros*, *Beyond: Two Souls*, or *Call of Duty*, dopamine levels rise with each new level or achievement unlocked. This reward circuit in the brain is critical to how people learn through reinforcement. "Activation of the pathway tells the individual to repeat what it just performed to earn that reward," says the Nestler Lab at Mount Sinai School of Medicine.

Learning effectively is about more than just understanding the material or being able to pass a test; it's an experience. With every successful attempt at understanding new concepts, the brain is rewarded with positive feelings, such as accomplishment and motivation, that make people want to continue striving for excellence. This cycle of reward and wanting to repeat the activity is essential in learning and having long-term success.

To truly make the most of life, it's necessary to take a step back from time to time and consider the larger picture. That's where this old adage comes in: "All work and no play makes Jack a dull boy." As adults, it can be easy to become driven by our daily tasks and forget about the importance of taking time for ourselves. If people can learn to inject a little fun into those seemingly mundane chores, tasks become more enjoyable and rewards make progress even more worthwhile. Crafting a balance between work and pleasure is an essential part of leading an enriching lifestyle.

Gamification works by leveraging the power of rewards and feedback to motivate people in completing tasks. It facilitates a positive learning experience, increases engagement levels, and encourages focus. With gamification, users are motivated with rewards that enable them to progress, complete milestones, and reach goals. This creates a sense of achievement and pride that supports ongoing engagement in spite of difficult challenges or otherwise mundane tasks. As dopamine is released during accomplishments, it makes gamers want to come back for more. Ultimately, this powerful brain chemistry helps secure desired behavior changes through the process of habitualization.

Gamification is an effective tool for transforming mundane tasks into engaging experiences. Here are some ways that can help gamify everyday tasks into something that gets the dopamine flowing!

Attach Rewards to Your To-Do List
Utilizing low-tech techniques is a great way to get started. For instance, **assigning rewards to a to-do list can help make the necessary chores feel more enjoyable**. With each task completed, you assign yourself points or another reward that incentivizes getting your list done quickly and efficiently. It's a great way to not only

motivate yourself but also involve the kids in the process, as it provides positive reinforcement. Get creative with novel mini games and see just how much fun tackling everyday tasks can be!

Rewarding ourselves for completing the to-do list is an effective way to motivate and increase productivity. Setting up a reward system that provides small rewards along the way as tasks are completed can help build momentum and determination by providing incentives for getting tasks done on time. The reward system could include things like taking a break from work, scheduling fun activities during the day, or treating ourselves with small gifts for hitting milestones on the to-do list. The key is to make sure that our reward plan is achievable and feasible; this will ensure that we do not become discouraged if the rewards seem too difficult to attain.

With effective planning, attaching rewards to our to-do list can help make it easier for us to successfully keep track of what needs attention while simultaneously keeping our motivation high.

Use Surprise Rewards

Implementing surprise rewards is an effective strategy for reaching goals and bolstering motivation. By writing rewards on pieces of paper and placing them in a jar, or assigning numbers to them and using a die to pick one, you can foster excitement about completing tasks or achieving personal objectives. It allows for the fun element of unlocking the reward, whether it's based on finishing a work project or following through with self-imposed goals, such as exercising for three days in a row.

To do this, set a goal or task to complete and break it down into smaller pieces. Once you have achieved each small section, you should reward yourself with something meaningful to you, like a five-minute break or the last slice of pizza. Soon enough, the anticipation of these small rewards will drive you to finish complex tasks more efficiently. Furthermore, surprising yourself with an unexpected reward after completing challenging tasks can help spur motivation going forward, as the feeling of accomplishment only increases with time.

Deciding on which type of reward to use is important, as this should still align with a person's overall objectives. Consider rewarding the progress made with something that won't undermine the progress made so far, such as a movie night or brunch date with friends once you complete a specified portion of the assignment.

Engage in Time-Based Challenges

Taking on time-based challenges is a great way to add an element of entertainment and focus to everyday activities. By setting a time limit and attempting to beat the clock, you can sharpen your problem-solving skills. You will be surprised at the innovative methods you can discover in order to beat your own best time. Doing this regularly will not only lead to increased motivation, but also improved cognitive abilities that can prove beneficial in any situation.

Time-based challenges can be a lot of fun; not only do they push us to take on a task, but they have the added incentive of having a timer ticking away. A great way to start engaging in time-based challenges is by picking something that truly excites you. If you're someone who loves cooking, why not try to make a delectable treat with the clock running out? Or if you want to tackle some coding or programming tasks, that could also be an enjoyable challenge! The important thing when setting off on any type of challenge is to remember that it should still be fun. So we shouldn't be too hard on ourselves and just keep going until we either finish what we set out to do or reach our personal goal, no matter how long it takes.

Make a Deal with a Friend

Making a deal with a friend or mutual accountability partner is an effective approach to staying productive and achieving goals. Setting a list of tasks to accomplish and creating an external deadline with consequences and rewards can propel both parties into taking proactive action for the day. Have fun by creating creative rewards and punishments; that cup of coffee or morning yoga session could be just the motivation needed to finish each task on time. By adding external accountability, friends can support each other in reaching their goals every day.

Chapter Takeaways:

- Despite having a broad definition, gamification really only refers to one thing: pleasure. The reward and motivational regions of people's brains are triggered whenever they complete a challenging task on their preferred app, whether it be a challenging word puzzle or a challenging exercise objective. This results in a fleeting but satisfying dopamine high.
- Implementing surprise rewards is an effective strategy for reaching goals and bolstering motivation. Assigning rewards to a to-do list can help make the necessary chores feel more enjoyable.

CHAPTER 5: DOPAMINE IS A LIFESTYLE CHOICE

Increase Dopamine Naturally

Dopamine is made by a small number of neurons, so any disruption can have a significant effect. Unfortunately, long-term stress drains dopamine levels and has been linked to conditions such as adrenal fatigue syndrome (AFS), as well as the symptoms associated with NeuroEndoMetabolic Stress Response. People with these conditions usually have significantly lower levels of dopamine, making them feel unmotivated and unable to fully enjoy life's successes.

Low dopamine levels can have an immense impact on how people feel, think, and behave: from difficulty concentrating and low motivation to a general feeling of apathy or listlessness. In fact, science has identified links between a lack of dopamine and a range of medical conditions, including depression, addiction, schizophrenia, and Parkinson's disease. That being said, it is important that people understand the critical role dopamine plays in terms of mental and physical well-being.

Low dopamine levels can have far-reaching consequences, as this neurotransmitter plays a critical role in regulating focus and motivation. Some of the common symptoms associated with low levels of dopamine include a lack of interest in physical intimacy (low libido), increasing muscle stiffness, difficulties sleeping, emotional and cognitive dullness, excessive fatigue, difficulty paying attention to tasks, apathy, and general listlessness.

If any of these symptoms are observed for an extended period of time, it is advised that individuals consult with their healthcare practitioner. While there are lifestyle changes that may help restore healthy levels of this neurotransmitter, specialized care may be necessary in order to ensure an optimal outcome.

The good news is that increasing dopamine levels in a safe, natural way will help alleviate most of these symptoms and restore balance in the body, allowing the individual to reclaim their sense of achievement and pleasure.

With increased amounts of dopamine circulating through the system, many reward behaviors and cognitive functions are enhanced as well. Improved memory, the potential to counteract depression, weight loss, a feeling of increased aliveness, impulse control, and addiction resistance are some of the unique benefits people can gain from increasing their dopamine naturally. Ultimately, increasing one's naturally occurring dopamine has been associated with improved cognitive performance while also reducing risk factors for certain diseases like Parkinson's disease.

When it comes to sleep, it's very important to be consistent. Not only does having a regular sleep schedule help people feel more rested and productive in the morning, but it also ensures people keep their dopamine levels healthy. Dopamine is a neurotransmitter that helps people stay alert and focused, so when they don't get enough sleep and the dopamine receptors in the brain decrease, their alertness levels significantly decrease too. This can leave them feeling sleepy and unmotivated in the morning, which makes it that much harder to get out of bed. So if someone is struggling with lethargy or grogginess in the morning, make sure that they're getting a good night's rest with as much consistency as possible; your alertness will thank you for it!

In case someone is having difficulties sleeping, here are some hacks that might help.

The Military Method

Developed during World War II by renowned military professionals, the military method is a process for achieving deep relaxation and sound sleep in a short amount of time. Popularized by Lloyd Winter's book *Relax and Win: Championship Performance*, this technique involves seven steps of physical and mental practices to de-stress and reduce fatigue. This method has been battle-tested over the years within the upper echelons of the military forces and is said to help achieve quality sleep in as little as ninety seconds. If there's ever a situation where someone finds themselves feeling overly tired or stressed, why not explore the benefits that this tried-and-true sleep method can provide?

All you need to do to get started is relax your entire face, drop your shoulders to release tension, let your hands drop to the sides of your body, exhale deeply as you relax your chest, and unfurl any tension from your legs, thighs, and calves. Even a few minutes of stillness can make a world of difference; clear the mind for ten seconds while repeating the phrase "don't think" over and over until the desired momentary emptiness is achieved.

The 4-7-8 Breathing Method
It's no secret that a good night's sleep is essential to overall health and well-being. The 4-7-8 breathing method offers an excellent opportunity to create a regular

rhythm of inhalation, exhalation, and retention that can help people prepare for sleep. The method consists of a five-step procedure that requires the practitioner to part their lips slightly while exhaling, inhaling silently through their nose whilst counting to four before holding their breath for seven seconds and then finally exhaling for eight seconds. This cycle should be repeated four times with the aim of leading a person into relaxation and ultimately sleep. Thus, by following this simple practice, it is possible to gain access to a blissful night of restorative rest.

Progressive Muscle Relaxation

Progressive muscle relaxation (PMR) is a technique in which a person tightens and relaxes muscle groups in a specific sequence. This causes the tension that was built up within the body to dissipate, allowing them to achieve relaxation and eventually sleep. To perform PMR, follow the below mentioned guidelines:

1. Tighten your forehead muscles by raising your eyebrows as high as possible for five seconds.
2. Relax these muscles immediately and feel the tension drop. Pause for ten seconds.
3. Smile widely to create tension in the cheeks. Hold for five seconds, then relax.
4. Pause for ten seconds.
5. Squint with your eyes shut. Hold five seconds. Relax.
6. Pause ten seconds.
7. Tilt your head back slightly so you're looking at the ceiling. Hold five seconds. Relax as your neck sinks back into the pillow.
8. Pause ten seconds.
9. Move systematically through the body—shoulders, triceps, chest, stomach, hips, thighs, calves and feet—applying the same tense, relax principle described above.

Practicing PMR is a great way to reduce stress, anxiety, and tension. It can also help improve concentration, focus, and sleep quality. If you are new to this or other relaxation techniques, here are some helpful tips for getting the most out of your first sessions. First, set aside fifteen to twenty minutes for the practice in a quiet, comfortable area with no distractions.

Make sure you're wearing loose clothing, as this will help you feel relaxed during your session. Within each session, start by tensing each muscle group for several seconds and inhaling deeply when contracting the muscle; exhale fully as you release the muscles into relaxation. Lastly, it's important to continue practicing PMR even in the absence of stress, since doing so will ensure you can better familiarize yourself with the technique over time.

LISTENING TO MUSIC

Music has long been recognized for its capability to move people and stir emotions in remarkable ways. Of all the senses, hearing has a unique ability to recall memories from the past with shocking clarity, allowing people to time travel into a different mental or emotional state. As it turns out, this phenomenon is partly due to the release of dopamine in the brain when listening to music. A study circa 2001 conducted by the Montreal Neurological Institute and Hospital showed that dopamine activity in response to music resulted in an invigoration of physical reactions, such as alterations in heart rate, temperature, and breathing. This explains why everyone is so deeply affected by music—because of how it impacts people on both a psychological and physiological level.

A variety of brain-imaging techniques were used in the study to track dopamine variations while listening to specific music. It was also concluded that this was the first time an abstract reward—in this example, music—caused such a significant dopamine release. The researchers discovered that five songs in particular, from a variety of genres, caused musical goosebumps and, ultimately, a positive emotional response in those who listened to them. These five songs have been demonstrated to promote happiness by triggering dopamine release:

- "Clair de Lune" by Debussy.
- "Adagio for Strings" by Barber.

- "Piano Sonata No. 17 in D Minor ('The Tempest')" by Beethoven.
- "First Breath After Coma" by Explosions in the Sky.
- "Adagio for Strings" in the version by Tiesto.

During the adolescent years, every experience is intensely emotional and unforgettable, strong enough to evoke powerful sentiments when revisited in later life. This emotional association with music is no fluke; the brain is particularly impressionable between the ages of twelve and twenty-two due to rapid cognitive development, and high levels of hormones further intensify the intensity of these experiences. In effect, when people hear a teenage throwback years after the event, it has an unprecedented resonance. Music cultures and styles change quickly, but songs we remember from the formative years can endure for a lifetime.

Music has always been a part of life, from the lullabies of our childhood to today's latest tunes. There's no denying that everyone experiences joy when they hear a song that speaks to them, and it's true—music can actually have an impact on moods. But in such a hyper-scrutinizing world, sometimes it's best just to enjoy music at face value, free of any assessment or analysis. After all, that heartfelt '80s power ballad or upbeat pop track can always be counted on to bring us some sweet moments of joy and peace no matter what else is going on in life. So the next time you want to feel good, why not put on your favorite record and bask in a downright catchy chorus?

DOPAMINE DIET
Everyone loves a nice sugary snack every once in a while, but what many don't realize is that when we eat those treats, our body can release a large amount of dopamine, giving us the euphoric feeling it's famous for. While that might seem like an efficient way to boost our dopamine levels and make ourselves feel good, it's not actually the most effective tactic. Health experts recommend trying out a dopamine-friendly diet instead, cutting down or eliminating certain food groups like coffee, alcohol, processed sugar, fatty foods, and carbs from our daily intake. But if we give this kind of diet a shot, chances

are that our levels of dopamine and overall health will improve significantly!

Tyrosine and magnesium are essential components to the production of dopamine in the body. These amino acids and essential nutrients can be found in abundance in nuts and seeds such as almonds, walnuts, pumpkin seeds, and flaxseeds. Protein is also necessary for stimulating dopamine production; therefore, lean meats like chicken; fish, such as salmon and mackerel; as well as eggs should be included in a healthy diet.

In addition to proteins and fats, fruits and vegetables play an important role in supplying the body with these necessary building blocks of dopamine; apples, bananas, oranges, watermelon, strawberries, avocados, beets, tomatoes, green leafy vegetables (spinach or kale), velvet beans (mung beans), lima beans, and peas are all good sources of these nutrients. Making sure to get enough of the right kind of foods can ensure adequate levels of tyrosine and magnesium for proper dopamine production.

Eating foods with high levels of tyrosine, like milk and other dairy products, is a great way to help keep dopamine at high levels. It's also beneficial to look out for other natural ways that can increase dopamine, such as through dark chocolate or green tea. Additionally, many believe that eating oatmeal or wheat germ, or adding some turmeric, can help the brain produce more dopamine. So if you're looking to give your brain an extra boost in the mood-regulation department, these are some tasty options to consider!

EXERCISE AND MEDITATE
Aside from increasing muscle mass and supporting the function of vital organs, such as the lungs and heart, regular exercise can also improve the brain's mental health. If someone has ever had a "runner's high," they may blame it on an increase in dopamine levels in their brain.

Walking is an excellent form of exercise that offers numerous benefits, from improving overall physical health to mood regulation. *Everyday Health* suggests walking as a natural remedy for depression, and it can also help those struggling with anxiety. With temperatures beginning to drop, it might serve as an opportunity to bundle up and go outside for some fresh air. Even if people have no access to outdoor spaces, walking around their home in the morning or evening can still be effective in working through negative emotions. Ultimately, walking can act as a meditative process by providing the space necessary to discover clarity and perspective, allowing us to approach our lives with more positivity.

If you want to increase the level of dopamine in your body, take up a variety of exercise regimens. Stimulating physical activity like barefoot walking or Pilates encourages the body to release dopamine, thus benefiting both your mental and physical health. Additionally, core conditioning and aerobic exercises such as swimming, cycling and rowing can provide further boosts to the dopamine levels in your system. Through these exercises, you will be able to support overall well-being both mentally and physically.

If you are feeling overwhelmed or anxious, consider giving meditation a try. It won't just help you clear your head and relax; research has also shown that it can increase dopamine levels! Increased dopamine signals pleasure in the brain and can be incredibly beneficial for mental health. Not only does meditation make people more mindful of their thoughts and emotions, but it can give them a natural boost of happiness too. So take some time out to disconnect from the world and fill up with some serious calm vibes.

This meditation exercise is an excellent introduction to meditation techniques. It's easy and intuitive; there's no need for any prior experience or instruction. All that is needed is a comfortable spot to sit or lie down, close your eyes, and focus on how your body moves with each breath. There's no need to try too hard; just let the mind do its thing without controlling it. You may want to invest in a meditation chair or cushion for added comfort, but that's totally up to personal taste. If your mind starts wandering, draw it back to the feeling of every inhalation and exhalation. And that's all there is to it!

CUT DOWN PROCESSED SUGARS

Consuming large amounts of processed sugars like candy and soda can give people a temporary feeling of happiness due to the increase in dopamine levels. However, this dopamine boost is artificial, as it is only a result of the sugar rush and not natural production. The rush can be similar to how alcohol and recreational drugs provide a false sense of pleasure, but it unfortunately leads to slowed down production of the body's natural dopamine. Eventually, this artificial rise gives way to a crash that leaves people feeling worse than before. To get back on track, people should decrease their intake of processed sugars and opt for healthier choices, such as fruits or nuts, that help naturally balance out the dopamine levels in the body.

After overindulging, it's important to take the steps to get off the high. Start by hydrating with plenty of water. Water will help flush the system and reset the body for a healthy start. Additionally, be sure to prioritize fiber in order to replenish what was misguided. Most individuals do not reach the recommended twenty-five to thirty-five grams of fiber everyday, so make more of an effort to fulfill this caloric requirement today. Lastly, everyone's plate should be loaded with lots of fruits and vegetables because they are high in water content and low in calories, offering a balance to our occasional splurges.

Last but not least, make sure that all of the meals include a solid supply of lean protein and/or healthy fat. Protein and fat break down at a slower rate, and when combined with starchy foods, they aid to slow the release of glucose into the bloodstream.

ELIMINATE STRESSORS

While there are external factors that can lead to stress and the related health risks, we possess the means to reduce our own personal levels of stress. Recognizing which activities or situations cause us stress, as well as healthy coping methods, are essential steps in mitigating potential harm. For instance, if you find yourself worrying while commuting to work, consider relocating closer to your place of business. Other activities like yoga and massages can also offer relaxation; sometimes simply talking out a troubling situation or volunteering in your community are great alternatives for easing stress. Finding out what works best for you and taking action is key in managing and minimizing long-term health risks associated with stress.

Knowing where the stress comes from is an essential part of taking care of your mental and physical well-being. Identifying your sources of stress can be complicated, as we are often not aware what causes us to feel stressed. We need to take a closer look, check in with ourselves, and pay close attention to the sensations we're feeling in our body. Ask questions like "Are my muscles tight or relaxed? Is my breathing steady or short? Are my hands open or clenched?" Answering these questions will help you become more conscious of any internal unrest and bring significant insight into which situations may cause you more strain than others. Allowing yourself to take note of any tension without judgment can aid in managing the stressful areas of your life.

Recognizing our sources of stress is the first step toward taking control of them. Once we've identified them, we can ask ourselves if there is anything that can be done to reduce or reframe our stressors. Perhaps we could try leaving for work early in the morning to help avoid rush-hour traffic. If conflicts are causing tension with you, it may be beneficial to set aside some time and practice forgiveness and compassion in order to resolve any issues. Being prepared ahead of stressful scenarios such as meetings or outings is also helpful in feeling more confident in such an environment. Lastly, don't forget to practice self-compassion by setting realistic goals and letting go of unachievable expectations for not only yourself but for others as well.

Being aware of how people experience and cope with stress can be very beneficial in helping to reduce its effects. Do you feel irritable or tense or have trouble concentrating when stressful situations arise? Do your thoughts become more negative? How do you manage that stress? Are your coping mechanisms healthy ones, such as exercise, mediation, or talking to friends and family? Or do they offer a quick escapism, like overeating, drinking excessively, smoking, or watching too much television? Paying attention to what strategies are most effective in reducing the stress you feel is key in ultimately managing it better in the long run.

Unmanaged stress can lead to unhealthy responses and feelings of defeat. Thankfully, reframing our attitude toward stressful situations can drastically reduce the physical and mental toll of stress. Studies indicate that if we view a scenario as an opportunity for growth instead of a drawback, we can avoid triggering harmful stress reactions. Additionally, adopting this outlook can open up possibilities in terms of clearer thinking and better control over one's physical body.

Adjusting Attitude

Stress can be a significant challenge in life, but it doesn't have to rule us. If we take the time to consider and incorporate these six suggestions into our daily lives, we can successfully reduce stress levels and more confidently navigate our way through difficult times. First, rather than view stressful situations as overwhelming, try to regard them as opportunities for growth. Second, accept that there are circumstances beyond your control—don't waste any energy worrying about what you can't change. Being assertive is key when responding to such scenarios. Additionally, tackle large tasks by breaking them down into smaller components so that the task doesn't appear so intimidating. Also, be sure to give yourself enough time when planning out your days and be ready for any unexpected changes that may happen. Lastly, a great resource many find helpful is cognitive behavioral therapy—a type of therapeutic approach used to identify and overcome problematic thoughts or feelings. By following these helpful tips, life's stressors can become easier to cope with!

PART 1B: HACKING YOUR DOPAMINE AND CREATING BENEFICIAL RUSHES

It's increasingly apparent that too much of certain things can be detrimental to people's health and well-being, particularly higher levels of dopamine. So far, researchers have identified coffee, cocaine, and other digital media as contributing to this imbalance, which ultimately results in a cycle of cravings, tolerance, addiction, and distress. The good news? People don't have to subject themselves to this harsh reality; there are ways to balance out these dopamine rushes. Doing activities like regular exercise or spending time with friends or family allows people to enjoy the positive effects of increased dopamine while avoiding any long-term consequences. So if someone is concerned about maintaining a healthy lifestyle while still being able to enjoy the occasional high, follow the below-mentioned steps.

Keep Track of Your Compulsions

Managing dopamine levels is a crucial factor in keeping a healthy lifestyle, and it is important to take it into account when consuming digital media. Too much dopamine can have detrimental effects and lead to addiction, tolerance, and psychological distress. To combat this cycle of highs and lows, we should seek out activities that create more beneficial surges of dopamine without leading to any negative consequences. Exercising regularly increases dopamine levels without any addictive effects, so it is a great way to find balance between the need for pleasure and the dangers of overindulgence. Additionally, taking some time for ourselves every day by engaging in creative activities or even just meditating can go a long way toward regulating dopamine levels naturally.

According to addiction specialist Professor Anna Lembke, addictive behavior exists on a spectrum; even if an activity does not fit the scientific requirements for addiction, too much of a good thing can diminish happiness. If someone's dopamine levels are persistently high, the brain may respond by reducing the number of dopamine receptors, eventually decreasing motivation and pleasure of any type.

In her book, Lembke recounts the case of a patient who became overly enmeshed in online shopping to the point of escalation. Upon reflection amid an ever-increasing presence of packages, he realized that what he really desired were those simple yet deeply gratifying experiences—the kind where one anticipates natural highs such as the excitement of anticipation to reunite with dear friends. Therefore, Lembke challenged him to abstain from online shopping for a full month. By taking this leap of faith and trusting her approach, his compulsion cleared up substantially as he slowly rediscovered "happiness" in every little everyday experience. Though for many others seeking similar treatment, Lembke notes how abstinence may not always be enough and sometimes more aggressive interventions are necessary, such as medication.

Get Some Healthy Pain, Be Wary of Combining Pleasures, and Meditate

By focusing on challenges that involve a bit of constructive, healthy pain, we can take advantage of hormesis—the biological response to stress—which can provide us with an improved mood and better motivation. This doesn't mean that activities must be unpleasant or distressing; enjoyable pursuits such as running cross-country or dancing ballet can all qualify. When people expose themselves to just the right amount of stress, it produces positive emotional outcomes. As Robert Sapolsky explains in his book *Behave*, "well-timed deprivation can do wonders for pleasure." By actively seeking out opportunities for hormesis, rather than hankering after unhealthy fixations and artificial dopamine boosts, this balance of pleasure and reward can provide us with a more sustainable emotional equilibrium.

While it's normal to combine activities to make mundane tasks more exciting, it is important to be mindful of combining too many pleasurable activities, such as texting, listening to music, and exercising. According to Lembke, the brain needs time when it is not being stimulated in order to appreciate the true enjoyment that results from any activity people undertake. Too much pleasure at one time can lead people to become numb or take greater risks than people would normally take, so enjoying pleasures in moderation is an important exercise for everyone.

Meditation is a great way to give your dopamine levels a healthy, natural boost. Eric Garland, a professor at the University of Utah's College of Social Work, created the program Mindfulness-Oriented Recovery Enhancement (MORE), which has been helpful in aiding those battling opioid abuse, chronic pain, and emotional distress. MORE involves teaching participants to process and cope with challenging negative emotions. Garland presumes "life includes triumphs and tribulations; mindfulness allows individuals to accept both outcomes while remaining in tune with their metaphysical alignment."

Boost Dopamine through Flow States

It's no secret that life can be difficult at times, but some people have unlocked a secret to contentment by embracing the notion that pain and growth often come together. This is known as flow states, and understanding this concept can help people unlock long-lasting feelings of satisfaction. Rian Doris explains that when people are so focused on a task they choose to complete, they go into a state of absolute focus, blocking out other distractions and worries. Miraculously, the body also responds physically to this constant focus, resulting in increased levels of dopamine, producing an overall sense of euphoria and joy.

According to Doris, leaving our comfort zones and venturing into the realm of pain and struggle is necessary to unlock flow. However, simply taking that courageous step is far from easy. Paul Bloom, an acclaimed psychologist, explains how "it's easier to sit on our sofa and watch Netflix" than take initiative for pursuing a goal. For example, if somebody wants to write a memoir, it takes countless hours of concentrated practice and dedication; it would be all too tempting for them to stop this endeavor in order to satisfy their craving for instant gratification. But with commitment and hard work comes reward. Running in the New York City Marathon gave Alexis the sense of freedom she was longing for while allowing her to zone out all distractions. Ultimately, people must expand their boundaries if they wish to experience those moments of sheer bliss known as flow.

Finding balance in moderation is key when dopamine is involved. Doris recommends not to spend too much time in flow, as work has become druggified like everything else for some people. Taking breaks with social media and video games can be a great outlet;

however, Bloom states that flow shouldn't be used as a cure. Rather, it should engage you in meaningful activities regardless of the struggle involved. By engaging in activities that bring both pleasure and genuine fulfillment with moderation and understanding, people can find harmonious balance that won't take an addicting toll on them.

PART 2: DOPAMINE AND GRATITUDE

When people feel grateful, their brain kicks into gear to produce dopamine. This means that by engaging in appreciative thinking, one can really experience a sense of well-being both chemically and psychologically. As this process is repeated over time, individuals are able to experience higher levels of happiness and health overall due to the increased production of dopamine. Therefore, cultivating gratefulness is an incredibly effective way to preserve well-being and positivity.

Taking the time to cultivate gratitude can be incredibly beneficial and can bring joy into people's lives. Practices such as journaling and reflecting on what they're thankful for each day, creating a list of accomplishments or things that went well that day, writing a letter of appreciation to someone who has positively touched their life, participating in kind acts directed at family and friends, or simply verbalizing their gratitude can help them appreciate the good things in life. Although it may seem daunting at first, implementing small daily bouts of gratitude practice can lead to dramatic results. By taking intentional steps toward embracing gratitude, people have an opportunity to increase not only their own quality of life but also those around them.

Sonja Lyubomirsky, a renowned positive psychology researcher and author of books on happiness, has demonstrated the power of gratitude for personal health and well-being. She argues that gratitude can act as an "antidote" to negative emotions and can help neutralize envy, hostility, worry, and irritation. This is because when people practice being grateful for the things they have and their current situation, it encourages them to be present-oriented and not take what they have for granted. Her research found that expressing gratitude can lead to more positive feelings and provide an impetus for self-improvement.

According to an article in *Wharton Healthcare Quarterly*, an intentional practice of thankfulness
can enhance neuron density and lead to increased emotional intelligence. Hebb's Law states that "neurons that fire together wire together" in neuroscience study. The more people practice thankfulness, the stronger the neural circuits in their brain for gratitude become, making it simpler to focus on feelings of gratitude.

Studies have found that gratitude can do wonders for mental health. It's been associated with increasing levels of dopamine, and recent research suggests it can also naturally boost serotonin—that "happiness chemical." In his book *The Upward Spiral: Using Neuroscience to Reverse the Course of Depression, One Small Change at a Time*, researcher Alex Korb writes that being grateful activates production in the anterior cingulate cortex. This can help people feel good and relaxed, as well as stabilize their mood so they're better equipped to manage difficult emotions. So if you want to reap the mental health benefits of gratitude, just take a few moments each day to recognize the things for which you're thankful.

Feeling appreciated and showing gratitude have been scientifically proven to be beneficial for people's mental health, and now recent research suggests that it also encourages prosocial behavior. Prosocial behavior is any type of behavior that directly benefits other people and promotes a sense of collaboration; it includes kindness, empathy, generosity, and cooperation. It's the kind of behavior that goes beyond just themselves and makes people want to contribute to society in some way. According to the study conducted by Dr. Newlin and Professor Newman at Stanford University, performing acts of kindness can serve not only as a self-motivator but also as an enabler of positive social interaction among groups. By extending their feelings of gratitude to others, people encourage them not only to help them succeed but also to motivate members of their communities to join them in striving for beneficial changes for all.

Researchers have discovered a connection between practicing gratitude and dopamine production. An influx in dopamine produces a natural high for the individual. Not only does it feel good momentarily but it also creates an inclination to return to the behavior that sparked that feeling of pleasure. In addition, dopamine strengthens the positive emotions one has so those moments may last longer. Consequently, when one feels good, they are more likely to spread their joy to others around them.

Gratitude Cultivation

Focus on appreciating what you have for TEN seconds

Taking a few moments a day to cultivate gratitude can have lasting positive effects on people's well-being. Research shows that reflecting on what people have to be grateful for can lead to increased levels of dopamine (Adler, 2005) and, thus, increased happiness, reduced stress, and numerous physical health benefits. To start accessing these positive changes, take ten seconds each day to focus on appreciating what you already possess—from the people in your life, to a piece of nature that takes your breath away, or even the simple comfort of having a roof over your head. Not only will this activity leave you feeling content in the moment, but research proves that it also strengthens mental resilience and encourages mindful living.

Receive gratitude by expressing it more often

Expressing gratitude can not just make a person more satisfied with life, but it can also have a great impact on the physical and mental health of both them and those around them. According to Dr. Huberman, research demonstrates that receiving gratitude has an even greater effect than giving it. One study had participants write thank-you letters to their coworkers and then read them aloud in the same room. Upon observation, neuroscientists noted a strong response in the prefrontal cortex of their brains, which indicated that being on the receiving end of gratitude is important and beneficial.

To ensure that you are regularly expressing your gratitude to all those around you, some steps you can take include recognizing your coworkers' strengths, thanking your loved ones, complimenting people you come across every day in a genuine manner, and taking time out of your day to simply let others know how much you appreciate them.

Create gratitude group activities
Establishing a gratitude practice among your peers can bring forth an environment of thankfulness and appreciation. As Dr. Brené Brown, a research professor, explains to Goop, her family demonstrates thankfulness through displaying kind thoughts for birthday persons and sharing what each member is thankful for at the dinner table.

Gratitude groups can be a great way to build meaningful relationships while reflecting on the positive aspects of our lives. The key to creating a successful gratitude group is to set aside that time in our schedule each week to give ourselves and others permission to express thanks for what we appreciate in our lives. To make things fun, creative activities can be incorporated into the meetings as well.

For example, use conversation starters or quotes about gratitude as prompts for discussion, share photographs of recent blessings and opportunities, play gratitude-themed games, create art related to the group's weekly theme, and more! When it comes to creating meaningful activities for a gratitude group, the sky's the limit! Creating group activities for gratitude is an effective way for individuals to show appreciation and foster a positive attitude within their support system.

Exploring simple practices such as heartfelt affirmations or random acts of kindness are some initial steps you can take in bringing more gratitude into your relationships.

Recall moments when you felt appreciated

Reflecting on moments of appreciation can have a profoundly positive impact on our mental health. In order to strengthen your sense of gratitude, it is beneficial to take some time and write down situations where you felt valued or respected. You can use this written record as a reference when feeling low or in need of new inspiration. Take a few moments to recall the emotions experienced during these moments and be intentional about savoring the feeling of being appreciated. Practicing this exercise is an effective way to increase feelings of thanksgiving and the associated health benefits.

Get inspired by gratitude narratives
Stories can be an effective and powerful way to increase feelings of gratitude. Reading or watching narratives about people who are helped by others or receive assistance from somewhere can ignite a sense of gratitude within people. The brain's neural circuits and chemical reactions become activated when people view these stories, helping them to empathize with the journey of the protagonist, appreciate the support they received, and connect with their emotions. To get the most out of their gratitude stories, break them down and really understand the struggles that were overcome or help that was accepted. Doing this regularly can be a

very effective means of allowing gratitude into your life.

Go for gratitude walks

Taking a solitary walk every day can be beneficial for your physical and mental health. Referred to as "savoring walks" by the Greater Good Science Center at Berkeley, this activity encourages people to take a break from their everyday life and focus on the little things that make up the world around them. During a savoring walk, consciously observe your environment as you go, taking note of sights, sounds, and smells unique to your location. At times, it might be difficult, but each step taken will help build within you a sense of greater appreciation for nature and all that is around you. Walk alone with intention and in gratitude; the world is beautiful and there are countless blessings to be thankful for.

Chapter Takeaways:

- Low dopamine levels can have far-reaching consequences, as this neurotransmitter plays a critical role in regulating focus and motivation. Some of the common symptoms associated with low levels of dopamine include a lack of interest in physical intimacy (low libido), increasing muscle stiffness, and difficulties sleeping.

- When it comes to sleep, it's very important to be consistent. Not only does having a regular sleep schedule help people feel more rested and productive in the mornings, but it also ensures people keep their dopamine levels healthy.

- Dopamine can be naturally increased by: listening to music, the dopamine diet, exercise and meditation, cutting down processed foods, eliminating stressors, and adjusting attitude.

- By focusing on challenges that involve a bit of constructive, healthy pain, people can take advantage of hormesis—the biological response to stress—which can provide us with an improved mood and better motivation.

- Meditation is a great way to give the dopamine levels a healthy, natural boost. The program Mindfulness-Oriented Recovery Enhancement

(MORE) has been helpful in aiding those battling opioid abuse, chronic pain, and emotional distress.

- People have unlocked a secret to contentment by embracing the notion that pain and growth often come together. This is known as flow states, and understanding this concept can help people unlock long-lasting feelings of satisfaction.
- Gratitude can serve as an "antidote" to negative emotions such as jealousy, aggression, worry, and impatience. This is because practicing gratitude for what they have and their current position promotes people to be present-oriented and not take what they have for granted.

Printed by BoD™in Norderstedt, Germany